'An utterly brilliant practical guide ↑
showcases the central concepts of aut
change: agency, collaboration, a
truly child-centred model for inclusion. A must read
practitioners keen to contribute to small world change!'

**Danni Lacey-Scane, Primary School Inclusion Manager,
Ashleigh Primary School and Nursery**

'A thought-provoking and reflective resource for researchers,
commissioners of services, and practitioners who are looking to
develop person-centred ways of working. It weaves together cultural
context, theory and key research, to present practical step-by-step
guidance to person-centred approaches that empower children to
participate actively in creating their future learning plans.'

**Claire Darwin, Principal Educational Psychologist and Visiting Senior
Fellow at the University of Suffolk (School of Psychology and Education)**

'This book links national policies to support children who have
SEND with the application of person-centred reviews in educational
settings, bringing to life the experiences of children, parents, school
staff and professionals. The theories and strategies described for
helping empower children and their families to work alongside
professionals in constructing personal learning plans are invaluable.'

Dr Shinel Chidley, Educational Psychologist

Personalizing Education

Personalizing Education

A person-centred approach for children with special educational needs

Nick Hammond and Nicola Palmer

 is an imprint of

First published in 2018 by the UCL Institute of Education Press, 20 Bedford Way, London WC1H 0AL

www.ucl-ioe-press.com

British Library Cataloguing in Publication Data:
A catalogue record for this publication is available from the British Library

ISBNs
978-1-85856-880-5 (paperback)
978-1-85856-887-4 (PDF eBook)
978-1-85856-888-1 (ePub eBook)
978-1-85856-889-8 (Kindle eBook)

Typeset by Quadrant Infotech (India) Pvt Ltd
Printed by CPI Group (UK) Ltd, Croydon, CR0 4YY
Cover image © Steve Debenport/iStockphoto
Figures 3.1, 3.2, 4.1, 4.2 © Katie Anne Speed (illustration and design) and Emma Heywood-Speed (assisting initial design). Reproduced by permission.

Contents

About the authors

Dr Nick Hammond is an educational and child psychologist registered with the HCPC (Health and Care Professions Council) and chartered with the BPS (British Psychological Society), a social theatre practitioner and a film-maker. He is Course Director of the initial training for educational psychologists at the University of East Anglia. He has been honorary lecturer at the University of Manchester's initial training for educational psychologists, has contributed to similar courses at the University of East London, University of Exeter and University of Sheffield, and has worked as an external supervisor to postgraduate education students at the University of Sheffield covering subjects within the broad area of international inclusion policy and practice. Nick's first book, *Forum Theatre for Children*, published by Trentham Books/UCL IOE Press in 2015, has received critical acclaim.

Nicola Palmer is a trainee educational psychologist at the University of East Anglia. She has worked with children using a range of inclusive and person-centred practices. She has worked in a specialist residential school for looked-after children, as a respite worker for children with learning difficulties and, most recently, as an assistant educational psychologist. In this last role, she has represented the psychology service within the Youth Offending Team and has co-led the research team developing a person-centred review model for children described in this book. Nicola is trained in solution-focused brief therapy and personal construct psychology approaches.

List of figures

List of abbreviations

ASD	autism spectrum disorder
CP	clinical psychologist
CT	class teacher
DH	deputy head teacher
EHC	education, health and care
EHCP	education, health and care plan (sometimes referred to as 'Plan')
EHCPCo	education, health and care plan coordinator
EP	educational psychologist
FSP	family support process
head	head teacher
IEP	individual education plan
LAC	looked-after children
MAPs	Making Action Plans
OT	occupational therapist
PA	parent adviser
PATH	Planning Alternative Tomorrows with Hope
PCP	person-centred planning
PCR	person-centred review
PSA	parent support adviser
SEND	special educational needs and disabilities
SENDCo	special educational needs and disabilities coordinator
SLST	specialist learning support teacher
SoS	Signs of Safety
SRV	social role valorization

Authors' notes

In this book, the terms 'child', 'children' and 'young people' are used interchangeably to refer to those from 0 to 25 years old.

The term 'educational psychologist', or 'EP', is used to refer to a variety of qualified applied psychologists who may practise under a variety of local and international titles, including educational and child psychologist, school psychologist and child psychologist.

Acknowledgements

This book is based on a major research project that took place over two years. It is the largest empirical study of the person-centred review (PCR) process with children, young people and their families within educational settings. It would not have been possible to undertake this without our extended research team, research partners and those who have supported us along the way. Both authors would like to thank:

- All of our research partners – children and young people, and their parents, carers and extended family members, as well as the school and college staff, parenting organizations and professionals from health, social care and education who participated. Thank you for sharing, and allowing us to share, your stories – without you, the research would not have been possible.
- Our extended research team – Michele Blazey, Lauren Boesley, Diana Metcalfe, Sarah Raspin, Helen Southgate and Frankie Stenning.
- Our talented artists and designers – Emma Heywood-Speed and Katie Ann Speed.
- James Thatcher, Keeley White and others who have supported the research into and implementation of PCRs along the way.

Nick would like to thank his friends and family for their continued love and support, as well as Gillian Klein for being an honest, generous and supportive editor and publisher. And to Nicola (Nikki) – thank you for being you.

Nicola would like to thank Nick for giving her the opportunity to be part of this research, which has led to so many new and exciting experiences. Thanks to my family and close friends for all their love and support. And to my close colleagues over the past two years, for their unconditional support and backup when I had too much on.

Chapter 1

Becoming person-centred

Today you are you! That is truer than true! There is no one
alive who is you-er than you!
Dr Seuss, *Happy Birthday to You!* (1959)

This book is based on a major empirical research study. Using a simple person-centred review (PCR) model proposed by Sanderson and Lewis (2012) as a starting point, we show the development and potential of PCRs for working with children and families within education systems and beyond transition phases. This book offers practical ideas and activities that can be used for professional, family and school system development.

Aim of the book

Like many people, we dream of the day we can change the world for the better – to create a place that is inclusive, tolerant, respectful and socially just. This world would celebrate difference, challenge socially constructed barriers that marginalize individuals and groups, and empower people to take ownership of their own destinies through genuine choice and support – uniting communities towards a common goal of living harmoniously. Some may believe that this dream is naively a 'big world' position. This may be so – the eradication of poverty, war and famine have long been attempted yet, sadly, they continue to flourish. We are not attempting to create big world change here, at least not directly; rather, we believe that big world change is the product of many small world changes. This book illustrates our belief that we can, through collective action, change someone's world – and that itself is quite something. This is the power of personalized education.

We begin with a personal story of person-centred learning. After reading psychology, I (Nick) undertook training as a theatre practitioner, during which I took a module in site-specific movement performance – where artists work on location, such as in parks or at the seaside, to create work. Two weeks before the final performance for this module, I was asked to present a work-in-progress version to colleagues and the lecturer. After the performance, I stood nervously awaiting feedback. After a short pause, the lecturer said 'if you were auditioning for RADA, I would give you a place without hesitation'. I was rather proud, yet I sensed a 'but' – and so it came: '...but if you perform that in two weeks' time, you will fail this module.'

That evening, I walked into a large, empty studio space, frozen by thoughts of how I was going to explain failing a module to my sponsors. My colleagues walked in, and we spoke briefly, and then they began to move around the space. They encouraged me to join them, and so, with some awkwardness and apprehension, I did. My background was in science – I was good at being in my head and not so good at being in my body – so I felt out of my depth.

I threw myself into it and, after what I thought was about ten minutes, I looked up to see that both of my colleagues had left. I checked my watch and, to my surprise, over an hour had passed. Two weeks later, I performed this piece and passed with the highest grade in the class. My colleagues' actions taught me three invaluable lessons. The first was how to play – perhaps the most primitive of human communication skills, yet one we are so often educated out of. This is a point to which we return later when we consider how to include children in their own planning. The second was that someone's perceived ability is not the limit of their potential when their teacher is patient, skilled and respectful of what they bring to the space – be that a theatre space, a classroom or elsewhere. And finally – and linked to this – was how to be person-centred. These lessons have served me well as a psychologist, and have influenced my focus on empowered participation. These lessons are shared in various forms throughout this book.

We unapologetically challenge power imbalances, advocate for social justice, and endeavour to champion the importance of placing children and their families at the centre of planning for their futures in a way that goes beyond tokenism. This book is based on the spirit of collective action, and the belief that everyone has the right to empowered participation and social inclusion.

How the book is organized

- **Chapter 1: Becoming person-centred.** This chapter begins with a critical introduction to personalized planning, and discusses PCRs in relation to other international models of person-centred working, such as Signs of Safety (Turnell and Edwards, 1999). Psycho-educational aspects of PCRs are discussed to reinforce the important contribution personalized planning can make to children's lives. We describe the sociopolitical context in which the research was undertaken, and offer a detailed overview of the research study that frames each of the following chapters.

- **Chapter 2: Experiences of formal and informal SEND processes.** Based on Cycle 1 of the study, we explore the views of our research partners in relation to formal and informal processes of supporting children with special educational needs and disabilities (SEND) in the UK. The chapter discusses challenges and aspects of good practice with an international relevance. The chapter explains why a PCR model was chosen, and how these ideas were integrated into Cycle 2.
- **Chapter 3: Preparing for a PCR.** This chapter focuses on the structure and practicalities of PCRs, and gives a step-by-step guide to running a PCR. Key issues are explored, such as the preparation and involvement of children, including those in the early years. The chapter is peppered with new resources, including storyboards, a child-friendly PCR report template and signposting to a child-friendly film that can be freely used by readers.
- **Chapter 4: Experiences of PCRs.** Built upon commentary from participants, and interspersed with critical theory relevant to the PCR process, this chapter reports the intricacies of the PCR process. We follow research partners who participated in a PCR, and explore the process and practicalities of the model in relation to children with SEND and their families. We consider specific issues, such as managing circumstances related to attachment needs and children in care.
- **Chapter 5: Summary and conclusions.** The preceding chapters are summarized and conclusions are drawn from what has been learnt. This includes consideration of where PCRs for children might be most useful, reflective commentary from the authors, key points to remember when embarking on a PCR and discussion of alternative person-centred planning (PCP) processes, such as Making Action Plans (MAPs) and Planning Alternative Tomorrows with Hope (PATH).

Critical introduction to personalized planning

PCP describes a collection of processes that can be used in developing action plans for a predetermined focus person – in this book, this refers to a child – and that are underpinned by a set of shared guiding principles that include (for example, DoH, 2001; Dowling *et al.*, 2006; Sanderson and Lewis, 2012):

- the focus person is directly involved in making decisions about his or her life

- power is shifted from professionals and services to the focus person
- the focus person is supported in reaching his or her aspirations by supporters – in this book, this typically means parents and carers, teachers, and external agencies, such as social workers, occupational therapists, and speech and language therapists
- the meeting is inclusive, for example, using jargon-free language, visual and interactive elements, and offering a choice of recording methods, such as writing or drawing
- the person's own skills, values and choice are central to the process, to create a greater sense of ownership and independence
- social inclusion is promoted by identifying access to community activities and positive relationships, to reduce inequalities.

Person-centred approaches have been revived following recent changes to special educational needs law in England and Wales. Although there are organizations and practitioners who use PCP approaches with children in education contexts, much of the empirical evidence, particularly that relating to PCRs, is often reported within the realm of post-16 and adult health and social care settings. This is problematic, as working with children poses a particular set of challenges. For example, the principles of PCP promote agency by the redistribution of power, yet for children this can be laden with problems, not least because there are limits to how far this can be achieved in adult–child interactions (Billington, 2006; Hammond, 2013, 2016). The complexity of agency may also be heightened for children identified as having SEND, due to the perceptions of some that these children are particularly vulnerable, and thus in need of constant care (Devecchi *et al.*, 2015).

The role of PCRs here is to help create empowering spaces within which children have an appropriate sense of agency. The child is provided with the necessary tools to share their views, and supportive adults are encouraged to be proactive in removing barriers to full participation by utilizing the child's skills and abilities, which enable them to reach their aspirations. However, supporting agency must always be balanced with the adult's duty to nurture, care for and keep children safe (Sanderson and Lewis, 2012; Devecchi *et al.*, 2015), and it is maintaining this balance that poses some challenges.

PCP in an international context
Person-centred approaches such as PCRs were initially developed in the US, and one of their early incarnations, Personal Futures Planning, has

been used widely in the US and in countries in Asia (Mount, 1992; O'Brien and Mount, 2005). The US has comparable laws to the UK, which aim to protect the rights of children with disabilities, such as the Individuals with Disabilities Education Improvement Act 2004. There is also an emphasis on holistic working with the family in the form of an individualized family service plan (IFSP), although it is not explicitly stated that this draws on PCP and holistic principles. However, decentralized policy and entrenched 'small government' means that there is considerable variation in US services for people with disabilities (Kirkman, 2010), particularly those of post-school age.

Similarly, Canadian education policy states that each child with identified SEND should be placed on a special education programme and given an individual education plan (IEP). This IEP should be coordinated by one teacher, but in collaboration with the student, parents, and wider school and community, drawing on external professional advice as necessary. New Zealand adopts a similar philosophy, although there is a greater emphasis on child participation. PCP principles and practices are also used extensively throughout Europe (see, for example, Lunt and Hinz, 2011).

Children's participation

> *NOW, what I want is, Facts. Teach these boys and girls nothing but Facts. Facts alone are wanted in life. Plant nothing else, and root out everything else. You can only form the minds of reasoning animals upon Facts: nothing else will ever be of any service to them. This is the principle on which I bring up my own children, and this is the principle on which I bring up these children. Stick to Facts, sir!*
> Charles Dickens, *Hard Times* (1854)

Structuralism is a philosophical framework that argues that human action, thought and experience are based on cultural norms, values, beliefs and systems, which are hierarchically structured. An example of structuralism and its relevance in creating change can be found in Charles Dickens's *Hard Times*. In this novel, Dickens captures the sentiment of what Paulo Freire (1996: 52) referred to as the 'banking concept', in which a child is deemed to be a blank slate ready to be filled with knowledge for later recall. It is a unidirectional process akin to knowledge dissemination, which can be found in examples of compulsory education within the UK and elsewhere. This social history and cultural norm are what we build all educational change upon, and these cannot be changed overnight simply by introducing new policies or legislation – cultural change is required.

Freire (1996) proposes an alternative education, based on knowledge construction, whereby children are encouraged to learn through active participation. The child should be enabled to draw on their experiences when making sense of their world and the curriculum, thus promoting agency and ownership of the learning process. This is a sentiment many educators will recognize, empathize with and aspire to. Yet, the structures that exist within societies do not necessarily allow for such change to be fully, or even partially, realized.

In order to move towards a system of greater child participation, one must first redress existing power imbalances in child–adult interactions and the systems on which these interactions are based. This is harder than it first seems. For example, the structures within which we live may lead us to make several assumptions based on cultural expectations. For example, education systems are typically perceived as being inherently good. Education is believed to have the intention of providing opportunities for social mobility and liberation – a generally accepted social norm value. In turn, societies act in a particular way towards education. But the education system could alternatively be seen as a form of social control. Education then becomes quite different: a system that expedites societal gain on behalf of the ruling classes (Boronski and Hassan, 2015), and maintains the social order through teaching and measuring accepted social norms. Coincidentally, this gives rise to oppressive SEND rhetoric (Allen, 2017) and maintains hierarchical subject values – such as the view that the sciences are more valuable than the arts (Robinson, 2006). Each of these examples has noticeable influence on how we act within, and towards, the education system, but also more broadly within labour and economic markets throughout the world. These perceptions, beliefs and conditions are intertwined into societal norms and values, which, along with child participation, cannot be redressed overnight.

Acknowledging this context from the outset is important for two reasons. First, meeting resistance to change, such as when implementing a new way of working, could lead the initiator to feel frustrated and helpless. We have argued that small world change is often the prerequisite for big world change. We might not be able to change societal attitudes towards the value of child participation directly or immediately, but we can, by using PCRs, allow a child to participate. Second, we take the ethical and critical position that it is important to acknowledge the historical and sociopolitical contexts within which systems are organized, and that give rise to the interactions that occur within those systems. This is important to validate the feelings of those who struggle to conform to traditional educational expectations, and have been marginalized through educational and/or social exclusion as a result.

Participation of children with SEND

The Geneva Declaration of the Rights of the Child (United Nations, 1924), originally adopted by the League of Nations in 1924, was the first recognition by the international community that children, including those with specific vulnerabilities, should be protected and included by the governments and communities of their nations. In 1948, this was consolidated and extended by the Universal Declaration of Human Rights (United Nations, 1948). These early incarnations of children's rights recognized the importance of the views of parents and guardians, and of promoting equality and equity between children. For example, all children were afforded the right to have their basic needs met. However, it was not until the Convention on the Rights of the Child (United Nations, 2018b), which came into force in 1990, that children were recognized as needing supported autonomy to participate in, and contribute to, decision-making that affected their lives.

While the protection of children's rights internationally has been progressive, domestic laws to provide adequate protection of participation rights for children with SEND were slower to evolve. For example, in England and Wales, the Education Act 1996, and later the Special Educational Needs and Disability Act 2001 – and the associated Special Educational Needs Code of Practice (DfES, 2001) – covered desirable aspirations in relation to the participation of children with SEND. Yet this legislation stopped short of making the participation of children in decision-making processes compulsory. However, the Children and Families Act 2014, and the associated SEND Code of Practice (DfE/DoH, 2015), moves beyond what adults *ought* to be doing with regard to children's participation, towards what they *must* be doing, so giving the participation of children with SEND special regard in domestic law.

However, as we argued earlier, cultural change is far more complex than replacing or introducing new law or policy. While new legislation may place an emphasis on person-centred practices, there is little clarity as to what this should look like, or acknowledgement of the intrinsic cultural and system shifts that are needed for an authentic person-centred practice agenda to be implemented.

Co-constructing individual futures
Towards co-constructed services

The construction of meaning and reality takes place in the interplay between the social histories and norms of the culture and the experiences, beliefs and values of the individual. The way we understand the world and the concepts within that world emerge, or are constructed, through the interactions we have with other people (Burr, 2015). In other words, our world is socially constructed, and co-construction of meaning and reality occurs between those afforded the opportunity to participate in a given interaction. This in itself is a theoretical argument for empowered participation. For example, we can imagine how differently a public service might function when the planning for that service is done by privileged experts – academics, politicians, professionals and so on – as opposed to when children, parents and communities are involved in that planning.

At this level of co-construction, we may be led to oversimplify: when planning services, we should ensure a wide range of stakeholders are included. Yet the reality is far more complex. For example, we must pay close attention to how those stakeholders are included, the culture within which the participation is taking place and the structures underpinning that culture. The concepts we use within our language, and how individuals relate to them, are also pertinent issues. For example, what might we mean by 'loneliness' or 'friendships', or even diagnostic labels such as 'autism' or 'depression'? While there may be a cultural understanding of these concepts – including diagnostic criteria – these may be experienced so differently as to create misunderstandings. It is entirely possible to hear what someone is saying, without truly understanding what they mean.

This is particularly important when we consider that our interactions are actions within themselves, as they establish boundaries and duties relatable to the structures within which the interaction has taken place (Burr, 2015). For example, a child who scores below a certain point on a standardized psychological test may be deemed to fit a specific diagnostic label that requires a specific form of intervention. This might lead to accessing a particular specialized setting or not being afforded equitable opportunities comparative to their peers, because of how performances on such tests are constructed. Critically, therefore, we must recognize the importance of inherent difficulties in our co-constructions, and not passively accept a trajectory of action that is akin to the social norms and culture to which that child belongs.

The importance of engaging children in planning for their own futures is therefore paramount. Hart (1992) proposed an influential theory, the ladder of participation, in which he argues that children must be given genuine, non-tokenistic opportunities to participate – ideally at a position where decision-making is a joint and active venture for all involved. However, the complexities of this endeavour are heightened by the skills needed to participate in the first place and, in turn, by the inherent challenges of co-construction. For example, while engaging children in planning their own learning objectives is considered a key task for teachers (Hargreaves, 2006), this requires the teacher to be skilful in proactively supporting the child to develop the necessary tools for engagement:

> Reality construction is the product of meaning-making shaped by traditions and by a culture's toolkit of ways of thought. In this sense, education must be conceived as aiding young humans in learning to use the tools of meaning making and reality construction, to better adapt to the world in which they find themselves, and to help in the process of changing it as required. (Bruner, 1996: 19)

We return to these issues later, when we share ideas developed by psychologists to support the eliciting of children's views when embarking on the PCR process.

Co-producing plans for children with SEND

The term co-production dates back to the 1970s, when it was used by Elinor Ostrom, an American economist, in an attempt to recognize and utilize the expertise of service users to optimize service delivery and development (Ostrom, 1972; Realpe and Wallace, 2010; Parks *et al.*, 1981). Since then, the concept of co-production has been embraced throughout the world and in all forms of public service.

In England and Wales, SEND legislation and guidance place emphasis on co-production of services, and on information being available for those who have, or care for, a child or young person with SEND (DfE/DoH, 2015). The focus is on reciprocal relationships and genuine partnerships between decision-makers and service users to create sustainable change (Cahn, 2004):

> Effective parent participation can lead to a better fit between families' needs and the services provided, higher satisfaction with services, reduced costs (as long-term benefits emerge), better value for money and better relationships between those

> providing services and those using them. (DfE/DoH, 2015: 63, paragraph 4.13)

Yet, as we have discussed, a change in legislation is unlikely to be enough to change cultural norms and attitudes. For example, Stephens *et al.* (2008) note how latent issues such as funding systems and the tendency of children to be defined by their identified needs are problematic. Attempting to create change in a climate of international economic, political and social unrest is challenging in itself.

Smale and colleagues (1993, 2000) identified three models of assessment, namely, the questioning, the procedural and the exchange models. Each model relates to the location of expertise, who is setting the agenda and the modes of information gathering and communication used. The questioning and procedural models situate the expertise with service providers or administrators. For example, the questioning model places the expertise with the professional – social worker, teacher, psychologist and so on – whereas the procedural model places the expertise with the managers or policymakers – service managers, SEND decision-making panels and so on. In contrast, the exchange model distributes expertise equally between service providers, professionals and service users who are 'experts in themselves' (Smale *et al.*, 2000: 140). Thus, power is exchanged within the assessment process so that it becomes co-constructed.

PCRs should place emphasis on co-constructed action plans where the child sits at the heart of the process. However, as Sanderson and Lewis (2012) highlight, the facilitator and those supporting the child must be able to move between promoting the agency of the focus person and making decisions on behalf of, and in the best interests of, the focus person. This is particularly the case when working with children and those who may require assistance as determined by the Mental Capacity Act 2005. Thus, simply accepting Smale's exchange model would be problematic in the PCR process.

Michael White (2005: 9), an Australian psychotherapist and pioneer of narrative therapy, talked of the 'therapeutic posture'. The narrative therapist must be able to move between prioritizing the stories, knowledge and aspirations of the focus person (de-centred/influential), and the statutory obligations and imposed policy, such as the Code of Practice (centred/influential), and assertive formal action-taking, such as initiating safeguarding processes and legal and ethical decisions (centred/non-influential). There is a fourth dimension to this therapeutic posture, which relates to non-action (de-centred/non-influential), although we do not discuss this element here.

White (2005) suggests that the therapist must have the ability to respond appropriately to whatever emerges in the therapeutic space, something he referred to as a 'response-ability'. The therapeutic posture and the notion of response-ability are concepts that can be easily applied to any process that is facilitated by a skilled professional, including PCRs. Chapter 3 looks closely at the complexities of facilitating PCRs and how these role distinctions can be established and explicitly changed throughout the process.

Beyond individual planning
The social value of children with SEND

So far, we have shown how society is a rich and complex tapestry woven together by layers of history, values, belief systems and norms. Within this, we have explored a range of implicit challenges that are often oversimplified when seeking a solution to a problem and, too often, overlooked. This brings us to a fundamental critical question: how are children with SEND, their needs and educational career valued by society?

We have seen a surge in equality and disability discrimination laws globally, yet families and young people with SEND often find it difficult to access long-term equitable life opportunities:

> The proportion of people with a learning disability who are in paid employment has decreased slightly year on year, from 7.1% and 7% in 2011/12 and 2012/13 respectively, to 6.8% in 2013/14 … there is more that could be done to enable people … to achieve paid employment. (DoH, 2014: 18, 25)

A more recent analysis of disability employment rates in the UK still shows significant inequalities in comparison to non-disabled counterparts (DWP/DoH, 2016). Children with SEND undoubtedly face a range of barriers to making a successful transition from education to meaningful, paid employment. We argued earlier that a child with SEND may be less likely to be afforded the opportunities to participate actively, given how their needs are constructed. Yet, even if we were able to mitigate the limitations to co-production and co-construction in educational settings, the value society assigns to a person's skills, and the constructions made of that person's specific needs, may not necessarily follow. And yet, paradoxically, this is also an intrinsic flaw of education systems around the world.

In England and Wales, it is anticipated that young people will typically exit formal education with no fewer than five GCSEs at a pass grade or above. The active discouragement of vocational learning, and the hierarchical structuring of academic subjects, has contributed to culturally embedding hierarchical values within the education system (Hammond, 2015a). We can see this in the science–art dichotomy, and also in the reduction of play-based learning, which has been greatly devalued. As Nick has described, people are typically educated out of being playful. Yet, play is intrinsic to much of what we consume on a daily basis, from technological advances to theatre, music and film. Education therefore provides the basis of what subjects and, subsequently, vocations and *people* are valuable for society, and this helps shape our cultural values and norms, impacting directly on the labour market and the skills that are sought after.

Clearly, structuring education hierarchically in this way reduces the value of skills that could otherwise afford someone access to the labour market. For example, a young person who is able to make themselves egg on toast is likely to be able to enter the labour market with appropriate support. They have shown the capacity to learn and to follow a process that results in a product – egg on toast. Thus, the capacity to learn could be extended and these skills could be transferred to the workplace, such as in a cafe. With a tangible value assigned to their skills, young people are afforded opportunities to acquire an income, independence and a sense of achievement, and to socialize with customers and co-workers.

The role of educators and policymakers is, therefore, not to determine whether academic or vocational skills are more or less valuable, but rather to support young people to do their best with the skills they have – in other words, to become more intrinsically person-centred.

Moving towards social valorization

The idea that every person has a valued social role in society, and should be afforded the opportunity to undertake that role, is at the heart of social role valorization (SRV) theory. Proposed by Wolf Wolfensberger during the 1980s, and developed through the 1990s, SRV theory is a central concept in critical disability studies and policymaking. The theory challenges the cultural values held about those who are traditionally devalued in society, such as those with learning disabilities. Wolfensberger (1995) argues that societal attitudes and values often lead to those with a disability – among others – being inherently devalued to a greater or lesser extent by individuals, groups, organizations, services and policies. SRV theory seeks to apply science to redress this balance by creating and supporting socially valued roles for those who are devalued within society, or are at risk of becoming so (Osburn, 1998). This is crucial because utilizing someone's skills within the workplace can grant them access to social, financial and psychological rewards.

Realizing the full potential of SRV theory is a long-term undertaking – it is big world change. Osburn (1998) argues that for SRV theory to be effective, change must take place at the level of individual, family, community and public services, and, ultimately, culture. While SRV theory is credited as being a staple in disability policy, the concept of disability and the value that people living with a disability have in society are historically embedded in language, perceptions, attitudes and actions (see Race *et al.*, 2005). Therefore, how we speak of and about disability is crucial in (re)shaping the social construct of what is and is not possible:

> ... if the ways of speaking about a young person are repeated often enough, it is likely that a way of professional thinking and talking will begin to emerge in which the young person might ultimately come to be viewed as synonymous with their behaviour, for example, '(s)he has behavioural difficulties' or '(s)he's autistic'. (Billington, 2006: 52)

We are moving from pathologizing towards normalizing, and from internal within-child deficits towards externalized needs that interact with factors such as the environment and other people. Thus, needs can be met through collective thought and action. Osburn (2006) argues that to create SRV we must both change the perceptions of others towards those who are devalued and develop the competencies of the devalued person through education, training and support. This is a complex business. Mann *et al.* (2016) found that current mainstream education is often complacent, and staff are poorly trained to meet the needs of children with SEND. Mainstream and specialist settings had culturally assigned (de)values that were embedded within the biases of parents and teachers. For example, where parents viewed their child as different, they wished to seek a specialist provision. The opposite was also true: parents who viewed their child as part of a wider society showed preference for a mainstream setting (Mann *et al.*, 2016). These expectations also significantly influenced what opportunities were afforded to the child in both education and longer-term aspirations. Thus, creating SRV makes it necessary to take account of the rich tapestry of the culture and systems within which the child lives (Osburn, 1998; Bronfenbrenner, 1979). Parents also need to feel confident that teachers are skilled in meeting the needs of children with SEND, and that their child will be part of a community built on an inclusive ethos that is seen in the perceptions, attitudes and actions of all those who belong to that community. We revisit this point in Chapter 2.

The role of PCRs
A historical context for PCP

PCRs have a valuable role in supporting the realization of SRV and, if implemented at the individual level with the complexities of cultural change in mind, PCRs have the potential to create big world change over time. How this can be achieved with children is the foundation of this book. In keeping with the notion that cultural histories are important for creating future change, we first explore the history of PCP.

The notion of including those who have disabilities in society, and affording equality of opportunity through developing services and conditions for disabled people, emerged during the 1960s (Wolfensberger, 1969; Nirje, 1969). Major challenges of the time included moving from institutionalization towards community services (for example, Kindred *et al.*, 1976) and the imposed limitations on those with disabilities, such as limited opportunity for learning and employment (Gold, 1972; Brown *et al.*, 1976; Bellamy *et al.*, 1979). The increased focus on promoting normalization throughout the 1970s led to the first, tentative steps towards PCP (O'Brien and O'Brien, 2002). Research at the time led to early incarnations of PCP structures, such as Getting to Know You, Personal Futures Planning and 24-Hour Planning (Galloway, 1978; O'Brien *et al.*, 1981).

PCP became commonplace by the mid-1980s, with the result that people were seen first, rather than their disability. At around the same time, disability activism began to pave the way for the discourse of a social model of disability:

> Disability is the disadvantage or restriction of activity caused by the political, economic and cultural norms of a society which takes little or no account of people who have impairments and thus excludes them from mainstream activity. Therefore disability, like racism or sexism, is discrimination and social oppression.
> (Oliver *et al.*, 2012: 16)

It is society that creates and maintains barriers that determine the extent to which someone is disabled (for example, Barnes, 1990; Oliver, 1990; Morris, 1991; Swain *et al.*, 1993). Individualistic models of disability also maintain a culture of dependency (Goodley, 1997) and so exacerbate social exclusion, isolation, discrimination and stigmatization. Researchers have long argued that practices must move towards self-empowerment, proactive challenge of discrimination, and environmental adaptations to support inclusion (for example, Oliver, 1996; Goodley, 1998). PCP therefore focuses on identifying the strengths of the focus person in order to raise their value in the local community, and to give them a voice in determining their own future (Mount, 1992).

PCRs in an educational context

The government White Paper *Valuing People: A new strategy for learning disability for the 21st century* (see Whitaker and Porter, 2002) outlined the need for change to improve the lives of those living with a learning disability. Key principles of this paper were to improve the rights, independence, choice and inclusion of those with learning disabilities, and to proactively engage people to participate fully in society.

Recent changes in UK education legislation reflect these principles, placing an emphasis on person-centred planning, co-construction and multi-agency working (for example, DfE/DoH, 2015). However, such guidance follows an adult agenda and so, by proxy, professionals are working within the aforementioned procedural assessment model (Smale *et al.*, 2000). This limits the extent to which one can fulfil the aspirations of true person-centred planning. A recent survey completed by the Association of Teachers and Lecturers found that 83 per cent of education staff felt that children and young people with SEND were still not getting the support they needed (ATL, 2016). Similarly, 58 per cent felt that children with an identified SEND were not receiving appropriate support to reach their full potential, with 71 per cent citing the new education, health and care plan (EHCP) system as a reason (ATL, 2016). A PCR in this context, and as outlined in this book, aims to equalize the adult–child working relationship and promote appropriate autonomy for the child. As discussed, we use the term 'appropriate' in relation to balancing the child's needs and age.

PCRs focus on what the child can achieve, while recognizing any limitations and systematically attempting to address them through collective action. By focusing on the strengths of the person and believing that individuals, and those living and working with them, often hold the answers to their challenges, we foster hope. Within education, facilitating strengths, resources and hope through the PCR process, we can encourage people to embark on challenging, yet profoundly rewarding, journeys of discovery and constructive, collective action:

> Person-centred planning celebrates, relies on, and finds its sober hope in people's interdependence. At its core, it is a vehicle for people to make worthwhile, and sometimes life changing, promises to one another ... Person-centred planning begins when people decide to listen carefully and in ways that can strengthen

the voice of people who have been or are at risk of being silenced.
(O'Brien and O'Brien, 2000: 8)

What PCRs are not

Meetings that take place in education and social care contexts take many forms but they all intend to bring professionals together to form an action plan that helps a given situation forward. Differences generally lie in the detail: how agendas are set, how the process is facilitated and the extent to which it can claim to be person-centred. Person-centred practice lies on a continuum that is more or less led by the focus person's agenda, as opposed to an agenda imposed upon them by professionals, policies or systems. PCRs and associated tools, such as MAP and PATH, are designed specifically to be person-centred with the child as the focus, moving away from an adult- or systems-led agenda. As we document in this book, we start and end with the focus person, which is not typical of many processes used in education or social care settings, despite rhetoric that suggests otherwise. We touch briefly on some of these processes here to draw some distinctions and address some common misconceptions.

Signs of Safety (SoS) is a solution-focused practice typically used in social care contexts to build on strengths within the family and provide an early help response to children at risk of safeguarding issues (Turnell and Edwards, 1999). Typically, these meetings are chaired by a professional who, through traditional round-table discussions, documents strengths and risks within the presenting context to draw up an action plan of support. While this is an extremely helpful and well-founded tool, it should not be confused with PCRs. For example, an SoS meeting is chaired, ideas are gathered through traditional means and one person records the suggestions of everyone – leaving any records or action plan open to editing and misinterpretation. SoS follows an adult-led agenda, with a primary focus on safeguarding. In comparison, PCRs are facilitated, not chaired, and ideas are recorded by everyone in the room, including the child, and can be drawn as well as written. In the PCR model shared in this book, the agenda is not predetermined, but equally, it is recognized that everyone will have their own objectives. The facilitator helps to bring all of this together in a collaborative, child-focused action plan that includes everything important to the focus person.

Meetings of professionals in education and social care are also a part of the family support process (FSP). This process aims to support a family that may have complex, multiple, systemic needs, or some safeguarding concerns. It allows for multi-agency working, so information is shared and services can be coordinated in order to provide the best possible support for the family. This is intended as early help intervention, with regular meetings to share information and outcomes of assessment, and to plan intervention. However, again, the process is traditional in approach, and is chaired by a key professional; although it is family-oriented, the child's views are not necessarily gathered prior to the meeting and the child is not necessarily invited to the meeting.

While PCRs share some theoretical basis with FSPs and SoS, such as being solution-oriented, there are important differences in the overall philosophical position. These approaches can be helpful in addressing specific concerns, but they are distinctive in many ways and should be used with a clear knowledge of purpose and alternatives. PCRs are grounded in social constructionism (see Burr, 2015) and critical psychology (for example, Fox *et al.*, 2009; Williams *et al.*, 2016). PCRs are based on humanistic principles (for example, Rogers, 2003) and personal construct psychology (for example, Kelly, 1963). PCR is a tool to engage in person-centred planning, and allows the facilitator to deliver a dynamic consultation. PCRs also share theoretical foundations with other person-centred planning tools, such as MAP and PATH, which are also designed to place the focus person at the centre of planning (Falvey *et al.*, 2000; Sanderson and Lewis, 2012).

The research context

There is a recognized need within the person-centred community for empirical research into PCRs in terms of effectiveness and best practice:

> This piece of work reflects our knowledge at the present time: it is not the result of a comprehensive piece of research to uncover innovative practice. Rather it is the amalgamated findings from a variety of projects ... (Murray and Sanderson, 2007: 8)

Previous research into PCRs has taken place primarily with those transitioning from child to adult services, and with adults with disabilities, generally in health and social care settings. There are some good papers available that report the use of PCRs with young people (for example, White and Rae, 2016) but they reflect issues with accessibility of PCRs for children, and focus primarily on transition. Having completed a thorough literature review, we believe that the research reported in this book is the largest empirical study into PCRs with children and young people who have been identified as needing, or possibly needing, support for SEND. We focus not only on the PCR process but also on how we can enhance accessibility for children through innovative practice and resource development. We also explore good practice principles for specialist groups, such as those with attachment-based needs and early years children.

The aim of our study was to understand:

- how formal and informal SEND processes are experienced by a range of key stakeholders
- how we might improve outcomes for children and experiences of families and professionals through efficient and effective person-centred practice using a PCR model
- how a PCR model is experienced and how it might be enhanced
- where PCRs might be best placed in existing systems and processes.

Earlier, we discussed our vision to support change of others so that we might build a better world for us all. Yet it is also true to say that real change starts with oneself. Through cycles of assessing a problem, planning how and trying out new ideas to overcome it, and critically reflecting on that process, one's practice can be developed – this is the principle of action research, the methodology used to frame the study on which this book is based. The lessons learnt from this exploration are reported throughout the book, alongside evidence of what works and what is less likely to work when rolling out a PCR model.

The research underpinning the book was undertaken by the authors over two years. We worked with over 60 partners, including parents, children and young people, and professionals from health, social care and education and parenting organizations. The study has three distinctive cycles, each informed and built on the previous cycle:

- **Cycle 1:** We began by discussing the views of formal and informal SEND processes with focus groups of parents and support professionals. We then analysed the data using a method called a deductive semantic thematic analysis (Braun and Clarke, 2006) and used this information to help shape the PCR model used, which was based on a model proposed by Sanderson and Lewis (2012).
- **Cycle 2:** The PCR model was delivered in a number of settings with a wide-ranging selection of cases. The youngest person to have a PCR was 4 years old; the oldest was in their early 20s. Needs ranged from social interaction and communication difficulties, such as autism, through to emotional needs, including attachment-based needs and children who were looked after by the local authority. All of the children had suspected or identified SEND.

A further cycle of interviews was carried out with parents and professionals. These partners were different from those who took part in Cycle 1. We gave simple visual-based questionnaires to the children and young people to capture their initial impressions of the process. We were interested in gaining better understanding of how the PCR process worked best for children, parents and professionals, while at the same time highlighting what did not work and needed changing. We wanted to understand in depth where PCRs might most effectively be used to meet SEND children, and where the outcomes might be optimized.

- **Cycle 3:** We presented our findings through an arts-based installation where partners could experience a mock PCR, view a newly designed pack of resources and a child-friendly film about PCRs – all of which are included in this book. We noted further comments by the partners and worked them into a newly adapted PCR model.

Chapter 2

Experiences of formal and informal SEND processes

If you always take it on the chin and wear it
Nothing will change.
Even if you're little, you can do a lot, you
Mustn't let a little thing like 'little' stop you
If you sit around and let them get on top, you
Might as well be saying
You think that it's okay
And that's not right

Tim Minchin, 'Naughty' (2010)

Experiences of SEND processes

The Children and Families Act 2014 and the associated Code of Practice (DfE/DoH, 2015) in England and Wales set out how a child's SEND should be assessed and met, and how these children and their families should experience them. Similar guidance exists across many international territories, including the Individuals with Disabilities Education Act (IDEA) 2004 in the US, the Disability Standards for Education 2005 in Australia and the Basic Education Act 1998 in Finland. Alongside other international agreements, such as the Convention on the Rights of the Child (United Nations, 1989), these govern how professionals should work with children and families in order to identify and meet need early, improve outcomes through effective cross-agency working and support children in education on a day-to-day basis.

However, despite these legal and guiding documents, systemic challenges can make the ideals difficult to realize (see, for example, Francescato and Zani, 2010; Williams *et al.*, 2010; Unsworth and Clegg, 2010). The *Pathfinder Programme Evaluation* (DfE, 2015b) was a national pilot in England and Wales that aimed to promote a smooth transition to a new system of providing support for children with SEND and their families. Although families felt a greater sense of participation and satisfaction with the new formal SEND processes, many felt a need to improve child participation and the range of support available in the local community, and to increase multi-agency working.

In this chapter, we show how parents, carers and support professionals might experience formal and informal processes. We identify challenges and aspects of good practice that inform the development of the PCR model.

SEND Code of Practice in England and Wales

Identifying and meeting needs early is a proven strategy for improving educational and social outcomes for individuals and communities (Allen, 2011; Field, 2010; Tickell, 2011). Yet, as reflected in this professional group discussion between an educational psychologist (EP) and an education, health and care plan coordinator (EHCPCo), current SEND processes may, at times, be used only to superficially meet a need that originates or is maintained systematically:

> **EP:** ... there are all sorts of issues; schools find the whole family support process massively time consuming and so some schools are resistant to doing it. You know all these things that were supposed to be there aren't necessarily there and that can cause a lot of pressure ...
>
> **EHCPCo:** There shouldn't be a Plan.
>
> **EP:** We totally agree with that. [It's] a knee-jerk reaction.

Systemic needs may not, of course, be limited to the school or social care systems. One extremely important systemic factor for a child is the family. Spratt *et al.* (2007) found that parents of children with SEND often experience high levels of stress, particularly where the child displayed challenging behaviour, while Carpenter and Egerton (2005) and Carpenter (2007) suggest that appropriate early family intervention can make a significant difference to improving outcomes for children and their families, thus potentially avoiding the need for overly bureaucratic formal SEND processes. We can see this sentiment in the SEND Code of Practice itself:

> A delay in learning and development in the early years may or may not indicate that a child has SEN, that is, that they have a learning difficulty or disability that calls for special educational provision. Equally, difficult or withdrawn behaviour does not necessarily mean that a child has SEN ... if it is thought housing, family or other domestic circumstances may be contributing to the presenting behaviour, a multi-agency approach, supported by the use of approaches such as Early Help Assessment, should be adopted. (DfE/DoH, 2015: 84, paragraph 5.29)

While the SEND guidance in England and Wales suggests that an assessment should be carried out where there are concerns that a child may have SEND, it must be recognized that one-off assessments of this nature are typically inferior to assess–plan–do–review cycles that take place over time. This is because the latter allow opportunities for information to be gathered, and hypotheses to be formulated and tested through well-founded intervention that is systematically reviewed (Kelly *et al.*, 2008; Beaver, 2011). This is known as a graduated response, and is emphasized as good practice in the Code of Practice (DfE/DoH, 2015). Here, a special educational needs and disabilities coordinator (SENDCo) discusses her experience of this graduated response:

> SENDCo: … in your mind [you] go through, if you keep it tight to begin with and then gradually you are opening up … so you start with your own professional skills within a school, and if you have audited everybody's skills you know if you have already got teaching assistants that can manage and if you have got people skilled enough. I think it is when you begin to look broader than that, and other agencies are beginning to say actually, I guess it is specialized …

When used appropriately, the graduated response is an evidence-based way of assessing a child's needs while reserving formal SEND processes for those with the most severe and complex needs. This targeting of services is essential to ensure that limited resources are used most efficiently and cost-effectively, particularly against the backdrop of depleted public services and continued austerity measures in the UK. However, local authorities must balance their statutory duties of due diligence in carrying out formal assessments with supporting settings to provide an adequate, evidence-based graduated response at point of referral. As one EHCP coordinator (EHCPCo) observes, formal SEND processes should be part of a much broader graduated approach:

> EHCPCo: … if we had done the graduated approach, you know, tried in school, we sourced external agencies we had looked to see what else was available to support the parents and the child outside school, tried that and seen no progress, to my mind it [the EHCP] is almost the last resort if nothing else has been successful.

We found that the experience of support professionals was largely that a graduated response was rarely followed:

> EP: ... assessment [requests] were coming through without any, how shall I say, without me having any knowledge, of the case, or the situation. The most acute cases were in early years; I could not see any signs of a graduated approach before getting into a statutory EHCP assessment request ...

In this study, children in early years education, and those with challenging behaviour and autism spectrum disorder (ASD) diagnoses, were the most prevalent referrals. It seems, as one participant pointed out earlier, that these circumstances led to referrals for formal SEND processes being started without much regard to other available resources. Yet in many cases a graduated response had not been followed. This was despite available evidence indicating that assessment over time is far more effective in identifying and meeting need than one-off assessment. It allows for hypotheses to be generated and responses to intervention to be tested in a collaborative and coordinated way (Kelly *et al.*, 2008; Beaver, 2011). In many cases, it is only after this process that one can accurately identify whether a child has SEND and provide a precise, evidence-based record of what is required to meet those needs. To this extent, unless there are exceptional circumstances – such as those children with complex and profound SEND who require access to a highly specialist setting and resources – a graduated response is the only way to make efficient use of limited resources. It is here that PCRs can be an invaluable resource for setting outcome-based targets and tracking progress with the child and family at the centre, thus reserving the often bureaucratic, time-consuming and costly formal SEND processes, such as EHCPs, for the children with the greatest needs at the lowest incidence rate. As these psychologists continue to reflect, support professionals have a critical role in supporting settings in undertaking a graduated response, to identify and meet the needs of children:

> EP1: I found I have quite an equal role there in creating that shared understanding of the legislation and process, you know ...

> EP2: Another thing that I have done quite a bit of is actually talking to people where I feel there doesn't need to be an EHCP. We have got together a few times and we've had a good plan and not gone ahead with an EHCP [request].

Guidance in England and Wales places an emphasis on assessing a child where there is a concern of SEND, but this needs to be carried out with some caution. 'Assessment' is a grandiose term encompassing a wide range of tools and approaches. The term has culturally embedded meaning and can vary between settings and localities. It does not necessarily equate with needing to use formal SEND assessment processes. The history and nature of the presenting case, the context of the child, family and school, and the questions that require exploration are all important factors in determining whether formal or informal assessment processes are most appropriate. It is inefficient, ineffective and potentially inequitable to utilize formal SEND processes simply because a child may have SEND, most notably in the absence of a graduated response and where context indicates far greater needs within the family or setting systems. Such an approach leads to a misuse of limited resources, and therefore to longer waiting times and potentially limited access to specialist services, such as educational psychologists, for the wider population of children who may benefit from systemic or group work offered by such professionals. Although not all formal SEND processes rely on a one-off assessment, many do, and this can move responses away from the true notion of person-centred practice and a holistic approach to meeting need, which in turn can reduce parental confidence (Lamb, 2009).

The Children and Families Act 2014 and associated SEND Code of Practice have strengthened the rights of children and families, placing far greater emphasis on participation and person-centred working:

> **SENDCo:** The [new] Code of Practice has been strengthened from the old Code of Practice, so instead of you *should* include the pupil voice, you *must*, and instead of you *should* include the parental voice, you *must* include parental voice. So, there is a lot more power to people, where traditionally the system has made them feel powerless ...

However, the Code remains vague and thus open to interpretation. While this allows for localized flexibility, it also risks creating inequalities in provision between children and families accessing support. So, ensuring systems and practices are in place that reflect person-centred practice is vital, and this includes PCRs that were run by the Educational Psychology Service in this study:

> **SENDCo:** ... I think that it is really good to make sure that [empowered participation] is embedded in structures in the way the EP service runs things – that they can prove they are attending to the Code. By making sure there are structures that are sound.

The Code of Practice places emphasis on local authorities to identify and publish what support is available to children and families in the locality.

Known as the 'local offer', it typically includes anything from clubs and respite through to delegated funding and specialist services. Children, families and professionals are able to access the local offer as part of informal SEND processes, and use it as part of their graduated response, to identify and meet individual need. PCRs could typically be used as part of the local offer, addressing need without the use of formal SEND processes. Yet not all systems operate in such a fashion, as provision available within the local offer is not always used in this way, as one deputy head teacher (DH) explains:

> DH: ... I had an application for financial support that I put in last term, one of the comments, one of the ones that was refused, was why had an EHCP not been started? So therefore, from a cluster point of view, I think there is going to be some weight if there is an EHCP.

Thus, while person-centred structures do exist and are championed within the Code of Practice, the document's vagueness leads to differences in interpretation and misunderstanding. In the case below, having criteria for administrating a delegated budget that relies on formal SEND processes was not only contrary to the spirit of the Code, but also created unnecessary barriers for the child and community:

> EP: There seems to be a lot of misunderstandings, which are carried over, and I don't know if they are particular to [the local area], but I think there are a lot of misunderstandings about how you access support for a child ...

Such localized confusion cannot be separated from the vagueness of detail within the Code itself or the context within which the guidance is being rolled out. As this EHCP coordinator highlights, a child's needs may be met within informal SEND processes – such as the local offer – while at the same time meeting criteria for formal SEND investigation:

> EHCPCo: ... even if you could say under the local offer that you can meet the child's needs and shouldn't need a Plan, if you compared it to the [formal SEND] criteria you would find that they could meet three or four of those categories, and actually you lost your argument ...

The *Pathfinder Programme Evaluation* (DfE, 2015b) outlines potential benefits and pitfalls for local authorities to consider when rolling out the SEND elements of the Children and Families Act 2014. However, it neglects the important role of localized context, so the findings may not be easily translated into practice everywhere. For example, some local authorities may be accustomed to addressing high demand for formal SEND processes by having a policy of high statutory assessment completion, whereas other local authorities may have criteria that specify exactly what schools must provide, supported by a robust school improvement service that can help facilitate a graduated response. This is particularly the case where a child's needs may become more noticeable or difficult to manage, such as times of transition or challenging behaviour, and should therefore be met within a setting's capacity. Formal assessment is, therefore, reserved for those children with high need/low incidence – such as those with complex and profound SEND who may require access to a specialist setting.

Accordingly, organizations must consider the context within which they are attempting to incorporate change. Mella and Colombo (2012) suggest a number of factors for which an organization must prepare, so that change can be sustained over time. These include the ability to think systemically and with foresight to sudden change, as well as thinking in parallel in order to consider the problem from multiple perspectives (De Bono, 1986). It is also important to be patient during the change process so that thorough evaluation and embedding can take place (Mella and Colombo, 2012). Impatience may lead to numerous pilots, and thus offer little sense of direction. When faced with the complexity of change, an organization must use the resources and adapt the systems it has to achieve a balanced process of change (Mella and Colombo, 2012). And, at a meta-level, the system must consider the culture of settings, and the support services, political agendas and communities they serve. These will to a large extent dictate how children with SEND are perceived, and thus how they are talked about and supported (Billington, 2006; Devecchi *et al.*, 2015).

Opportunities of formal SEND

Formal SEND processes have their place. As this parent describes, in her experience, the EHCP accurately identified her child's needs and allowed her to access the most appropriate provision to meet those needs:

> **Parent:** We now have a document that really describes him … he is now at a different college and very happy, and the EHCP took him there because it described who he was …

Here, a health-based clinical psychologist (CP) describes how parents are encouraged to request formal SEND processes following an ASD diagnosis to support transition to school:

> CP: … like I say, when children are transferring into school, a lot of the children in the last year have been applying for EHCPs … I always get asked for existing reports and sometimes get asked for current reports as well, which is sometimes a little trickier because sometimes as I haven't seen them since diagnosis and that's basically been the involvement in sending in the reports and encouraging parents to apply.

Following a diagnosis of ASD, most children have already had an extensive assessment, and, as this psychologist notes, a request for an EHCP does not usually secure additional information. Moreover, the legitimacy of using formal SEND processes for transition is questionable, particularly as informal processes such as PCRs are likely to be sufficient in managing the process. Keenan *et al.* (2010) suggest that a diagnosis of ASD was a precursor to a request for formal SEND assessment. We found a similar pattern in our study. While formal assessment will be appropriate in some cases, a significant proportion of requests appear to be diagnosis-driven as opposed to needs-driven. This is a pattern akin to a medical model of working – one that can maintain dependency (Goodley, 1997). Furthermore, many parents felt the outcome of formal assessment did not reflect need or provision accurately (Keenan *et al.*, 2010). In contrast, by adopting a social model of disability, we not only become more person-centred but also move away from considering within-child deficits and towards inclusive practices (Barnes, 1990; Oliver, 1990, 1996; Morris, 1991; Swain *et al.*, 1993; Goodley, 1998; Oliver *et al.*, 2012).

Nevertheless, formal SEND processes should also include a post-assessment, multi-agency planning meeting, which is often thought to be the most beneficial aspect, as this psychologist observes:

> EP: … I have actually achieved fantastic Plans in relatively little time, and so for me often, you know, when you think about the time and input that we put in to the assessment process and report writing and to actually make it more possible for us to be able to engage with the process of meetings would, to me, makes much more sense because I have often felt that so much of what I write is background – there is a lot of stuff, yes it is useful, but it is not necessarily essential, but what is essential is the Plan …

The Code of Practice aims to achieve this form of person-centred and outcome-focused working in order to generate personalized plans to meet need. However, this kind of planning, where appropriate to the case, could be achieved through a PCR for more children, within a shorter time frame and at a significantly reduced cost when formal processes are not necessary. The success of using PCRs in this way will depend on both the case and what formal SEND processes are designed to achieve in each local authority. For example, where an EHCP is linked to accessing funding or specialist provision, formal processes will always be necessary, but where formal processes have been initiated due to transition or high adult anxiety, for example, PCRs are likely to be more suitable. These issues are discussed further in Chapter 3.

Where formal SEND processes are appropriate, the Children and Families Act 2014 places a greater emphasis on child participation, and this can provide an excellent opportunity for professionals to engage these often-salient voices, as this parent highlights:

> **Parent:** It is very clear your child gets a voice, which I think is particularly important for the child.

Where formal processes are coordinated by skilled and sensitive professionals, the experience can feel very much family-centred:

> **EP:** ... the meetings I have gone to have been very positive and ... one thing I would really credit the EHCP coordinators I worked with, engaged parents really brilliantly in the meetings and felt they really made it very clear that it is a parental meeting ... it is very much focused on the parent and very much the questions are directed at the parent, and you know the information and so on, and so I felt very much that the parents have come out of those meetings feeling wow, they have been listened to, they have had their chance ...

> **Parent:** ... one of the things that is great about the EHCP is that I asked my son to write down under headings things like where he saw himself living and, you know, I didn't even know he had thought about this stuff, you know, it is hard to have that sort of conversation with him, but he wrote down 'I see myself living in a flat with a friend who has got some problems the same as me but is a bit cleverer'. But I thought that says everything, it says he doesn't see himself as being cared for, in a, you know, but I do know I need a bit of, you know, support and, you know, he has got a grip of where he is at, but by having this in writing I can help him to get there; we can't do it if it's just an idea floating about.

Although this mother describes an elicitation activity of her own initiative, the formal SEND process created a space for this conversation and a vehicle by which her son's views could be advocated. In Chapter 4, we explore eliciting views as a key preparation activity for PCRs and share ideas of how it can be achieved with both verbal and non-verbal children and young people.

Practical issues of formal SEND

The Children and Families Act 2014 reduced the time within which formal SEND assessments should be completed from 26 weeks to 20. The preliminary *Pathfinder Programme Evaluation* (Spivack *et al.*, 2014) highlighted that during trials these timings were problematic, and pointed to some potential solutions, including strengthening multi-agency working, information sharing and alignment of systems and processes. However, many parents still report experiencing long delays:

> **Parent:** The only thing I would say is that it was a long process for us because it started at the school [but] school was only interested in getting him into the next stage at college and so it meant they were very focused ...

> **Parent:** But the process takes too long then, so you are between a rock and a hard place now because the process is going to take you so long to get your diagnosis but you have to make your applications now, and because of that you have to do it that little bit earlier as well, and the [formal SEND] process takes, can take, they say, six months, but you know by the time you have had three rejections you are three years down the line.

These parents note that delays are still prevalent. Despite pilots showing that delays were likely, and indications of how they might be overcome, parents continue to experience such challenges. There appear to be issues of fragmented and short-term thinking around long-term needs and the challenges faced when systems do not align – such as admissions, diagnostic and SEND assessment processes. Fragmentation and non-alignment of services create challenges for the professionals operating within the system and for clients receiving education, health and social care services. Such shortfalls affect relationships between parents, settings and the local authority:

> **EHCPCo:** I have had some positive comments back from parents, that our biggest difficulty is being the delay, timescales.

> Sometimes we have negative effects because it has meant that
> a late request for a special school … it is difficult because you
> know it does affect how you, your relationships with schools,
> your relationships with parents …

Throughout this study, we found a high degree of circular attribution
between parents, support professionals, the local authority and schools.
Attribution theory is concerned with the information that individuals use to
understand the outcome of an event (Fiske and Taylor, 1991):

> An effect is attributed to the one of its possible causes with which
> over time it covaries. The principle applies when the attributor
> has information about the effect at two or more points in time.
> (Kelley, 1973: 108)

Heider (1958) proposed the theory of the 'naive psychologist', whereby
individuals look for causes to understand their own and others' behaviour.
From observation, Heider posited two ideas: internal and external
attribution. Internal attribution locates the cause of a phenomenon within
internal factors, such as individual personality traits. External attribution
locates the cause within external factors that fall beyond the individual's
control, such as environment, systems or other people. Attribution becomes
circular when two or more parties – such as parents and setting – each
place responsibility for a phenomenon within a given situation – such as
a child's challenging behaviour – on the other. In our study, for example,
many parents felt they needed to fight for their child against a setting that
would not engage, and a system that has progressively lost its influence
since power was devolved from local government to schools, most notably
by academization:

> **Parent:** Then there is the other school where, excuse me, you have
> special needs – forget it. I know I have had experience with one
> of those schools where, you know, the SENDCo is about this big
> and a new cluster [of schools] that never does anything, never
> follows anything up. But how the hell do you fight then because
> each one is a unit in itself, the council cannot go in and go 'oh –
> you are a local authority school, therefore you will', all they can
> do is, say 'you ought, you ought'…

Settings typically claimed that information from the local authority was
unclear, whereas support professionals, as we saw, argue that settings

did not always follow SEND protocols, such as an appropriate graduated response.

Weiner (1979, 1985, 1986) developed the idea of attribution further. He suggested that when individuals make attributions to outcomes, they consider three factors: locus of causality (internal or external), stability and controllability (Hogg and Vaughan, 2013). Locus of causality is concerned with locating the cause either internally – I did not achieve the desired outcome from formal SEND processes because I did not complete the appropriate graduated response; or externally – I did not achieve the desired outcome from formal SEND processes because the systems are unsupportive. Controllability is the amount of control an individual has over the outcome. For example, a setting can control how well it gathers and documents evidence of a graduated response. Even if this is an area of development, there are services the setting can engage with to improve. However, the setting cannot control the criteria or decision-making process set by the local authority, nor changes to SEND guidance from central government. Finally, stability describes the cause as either temporary or stable. Attribution theory is beneficial in the field of SEND as it provides a theoretical framework for understanding how individuals make sense of outcomes for children, and the interactive aspects of those views. In turn, all those involved are better placed to gain deeper understanding of multi-perspectives and by doing so negotiate a mutually satisfactory, person-centred plan to move forward.

Limitations of formal SEND
Whether a plan is derived through formal or informal SEND processes, the way systems are set up to mediate the implementation of the plan is crucial to earning parents' confidence. However, not every plan is successfully implemented, even when it is based on SEND legislation:

> **Parent 1:** That's what really annoys me if you look at the Children and Families Act, right, Code of Practice, 275 pages, you read it and it is fabulous and, right, you think, how wonderful, but the one bit missing it is called 'accountability' – how the hell do you screw somebody who doesn't do what it is legally required to do, there is no way of doing it.

> **Parent 2:** They aren't even getting compliant at all.

> **Parent 1:** No.

These parents share their frustration that, despite the improvements of recent SEND changes in England and Wales, there appears to be little scope for them to enforce their rights. We found a general sense that the Children and Families Act 2014 affords a level of protection and rights that is not provided elsewhere. However, in England and Wales, there is provision outside this legislation that allows for redress. For example, the Equality Act 2010 prevents settings from acting in a way that would discriminate on grounds of disability – among other characteristics. Many local authorities also offer families and settings mediation, school improvement services and other localized processes to ensure the needs of children are met. But the greater choice, and the devolution of power to settings, makes it far harder for local authorities to hold settings directly accountable, despite the proviso that local authorities should act as advocates for high educational standards. The limits to SEND legislation also mean that while the process is intended to be multidisciplinary, ultimate responsibility to participate falls to education services:

> **EHCPCo:** I think that some parents' perception was with the Plan we can say that health must do this and social care must give respite, and we have said 'no', if you get it, and if they allow us to, we can put it in the Plan.

> **Parent adviser (PA):** So quite a dark title for something that it isn't doing what it says on the tin.

While parents are led to believe that formal SEND processes lead to a coordinated multi-agency Plan that could allow them to access resources, this is rarely the case. Locally to this study, as in many parts of the UK, financial resources for children with SEND are already delegated to schools. These form a key part of the core and local offers. At the point of an EHCP being issued, children, young people and families have the possibility of accessing a specialist setting and, if the child and circumstances meet specified local criteria, a personal budget. Yet, importantly, a local authority is under no duty to provide a personal budget (DfE/DoH, 2015). In addition, even where a formal SEND assessment is agreed by the local authority, as this EHCP coordinator highlights, it does not necessarily lead to any greater coordinated or multi-agency response:

> **EHCPCo:** We have not really been having the reports or the confirmation, and the health part would really have to be signed off by health and they are not yet writing reports, even if a child is on medication or seeing a paediatrician or clinical psychologist,

we have not yet had enough where we can write that in, all we can do is summarize and bullet points for this child.

At the time of our study, it was common practice for health colleagues to recommend formal SEND assessment but not to engage with the process, seeing it as a concern that belongs to education. This misunderstanding of when formal SEND processes should be used is endemic, and a concern that has anecdotally occurred in localities across the UK. In this case, the EHCP coordinator reflects that inadequate understanding of the process and lack of engagement have led to delayed health commentary, and sometimes no health commentary at all, and thus a depleted final assessment report. While there is certainly a drive not to duplicate work when assessments exist already, this level of engagement is far from the spirit of the Code of Practice in relation to multidisciplinary responses to meeting the SEND of children (DfE/DoH, 2015):

> PA: ... I think that is quite a big disappointment for lots of families, particularly with the more complex youngsters. They thought back to that feeling of power they have got with this piece of paper, they thought that it would be written down, what I can expect from health, social care colleagues. The reality of the ones I have seen so far, from the families who have spoken with me, hasn't really got that there. Yes, it has got the aspirations but they are around learning ... it is not the whole Plan that they were hoping for.

One must pause to reflect on why this might be. It is certainly true that ongoing austerity measures in the UK have stretched public services to an unprecedented degree. And aligning complex education, health and social care systems poses challenges – and highlights another pertinent finding of our study: the need for awareness and skills training for the SEND workforce.

Need for a skilled workforce

As we have seen, some parents are encouraged to request assessment through formal SEND processes, believing these are necessary when this may not be the case. We found a lot of misunderstanding about these processes in our study:

> EHCPCo: That's interesting, just from being around school the phrase I've heard repeated several times was if you get the parent to fill in their form, they are more likely to get the Plan.

> **EP:** The other misunderstanding about it is that notion that [you have] got to be thinking ahead. Loads of people have said to me 'oh yes, I know they don't have any problems now but just think about transfer, or just think about this or what will happen when that happens'. I think that is a real big misunderstanding ... they were never meant to be planning ahead, people do have a particular panic around primary–high [school transition] ...

The psychologist here reflects the tensions felt at times of change, and particular pressure points in the system for formal SEND requests. Transition makes many children and families anxious, particularly when the child has additional needs (for example, Connolly and Gersch, 2016; Lightfoot and Bond, 2013; West *et al.*, 2010). However, transitions are typically made successfully, and there are many effective person-centred approaches to manage times of change (for example, Neal and Frederickson, 2016; Hammond, 2015a, 2015b; Jindal-Snape *et al.*, 2011; Deuchar, 2009; Evangelou *et al.*, 2008; Jindal-Snape and Foggie, 2008; Dockett and Perry, 2007; Sirsch, 2003). Despite the existing evidence base, parents can often feel confused, anxious and keen to maintain strategies that may not be useful for the child in a different setting or for long-term learning outcomes:

> **CP:** I think parents think there is a lot of confusion out there, actually.
>
> **Interviewer:** Right.
>
> **CP:** ... I think it is really muddled. I think where parents have a really good relationship with the nursery the children are already in, and where they have a good relationship with the school they are going to, I think it goes smoother. I think where parents ... are very [much] hoping and assuming, because their child got one-to-one [support] at nursery, that they are assuming they will get one-to-one at school and then realize that very well may not be the case ...

Although receiving evidence-based and targeted additional support in school can be transformative for children, there is no evidence that one-to-one support for children with SEND is an effective strategy. It may even have negative effects on progress (Sharples *et al.*, 2015). In exceptional circumstances, such as where the child's needs pose a serious risk of harm to themselves or others, there may well be a need for full-time, or almost full-time, one-to-one support in a school setting. Otherwise, any additional support identified should be managed through a key-worker arrangement, rather than one-to-one. For example, some children with certain emotional needs may benefit from someone who can offer support flexibly, such as throughout the day, at a time of transition (for example, Bomber, 2007; Geddes, 2005), while some children experiencing ASD may benefit from having consistency in the adult support when required. In early years settings, it is accepted that assigning a key person to every child is a valuable aspect of the education and care being offered (Elfer *et al.*, 2012). However, this may increase a parent's anxiety for a child who has SEND at times of transition, leading the parent to assume that such support will continue and is needed when the child moves to primary school. It is important to manage parental expectations by providing information on developmental stages and how support is provided across different education settings. Moreover, as affirmed by the attachment theories on which the principles of the key person are based, it is preferable to provide a developmentally sensitive process by which the child is encouraged to move healthily between reliance and self-reliance. To achieve this, they must first learn that adults are trustworthy and accessible, so they can build their capacity to hold these secure relationships in mind while they are separated from the caregiver (see, for example, Schofield and Beek, 2006; Bowlby, 2005):

> ... human beings of all ages are happiest and able to deploy their talents to best advantage when they are confident that, standing behind them, there are one or more trusted persons who will come to their aid should difficulties arise. (Bowlby, 2005: 124–5)

The concept of mind-mindedness (Meins, 1997) builds on this idea. Here, a caregiver provides attention and sensitive feedback to the child about their needs, wishes and feelings from the child's perspective (Schofield and Beek, 2006). This allows the child to learn and become empathetic to the needs of others, and at the same time helps them to trust their own emotions and thoughts, and so begin becoming appropriately self-reliant (Schofield and Beek, 2006). These are developmentally important aspects of early years education and, for children with some SEND, having a key person providing this support over a longer period of time is helpful.

Yet, when a child has SEND, we may be culturally more inclined to overcompensate for the perceived vulnerabilities they present, and so run the risk of undervaluing their competence (Devecchi *et al.*, 2015). Careful management is required so that anxieties are not colluded with, because the (best-intentioned) provision of one-to-one support may become counterproductive. Children with SEND are likely to need a robust transition plan that can contain adult anxieties while facilitating an action plan to empower the child to fulfil their potential. PCRs have often been effectively used in this way, particularly for young people moving into adulthood (Sanderson and Lewis, 2012). Yet, as the psychologist above noted, relationships and confidence that a child's needs will be met are equally important factors:

> **Parent:** ... it was important to me, that my children went to mainstream school because I see them as a whole part of the world not just a little bit of the world. But certainly, when I took my daughter who has Down's syndrome [for a primary school visit], and that was quite obvious she is going to have issues, you know it is not a difficult thing for people to establish ... the SENDCo said would I like to come in for a morning to see how impossible it would be? I said, 'no thank you very much'. We went to a different school.

The Carter Review (DfE, 2015a) found that there were significant gaps in initial teacher training (ITT) courses on assessment, behaviour management and SEND. Potentially this can be a serious barrier to securing a skilled workforce who can meet a wide range of needs in mainstream settings. Stephens *et al.* (2004) carried out a comparative study into teacher training in the UK and Norway, which revealed some interesting differences in the expectations set for education providers. For example, in Norway, trainee teachers are explicitly taught how to differentiate for mixed-ability groups and have a clear focus on inclusive education. In the UK, meeting the needs of children with SEND is seen as a legal responsibility and only referred to very lightly within teacher standards (DfE, 2011) In Norway, on the other hand, teaching is considered a caring profession where meeting the educational needs of a child is framed within moral duties and guidance that are akin to attachment principles, such as being accessible and trusted as reliable when the child needs help and support (Stephens *et al.*, 2004). Thus, there are issues not only over providing a skilled workforce, but also about the standards that govern how children with SEND fundamentally experience education. We found that parents in our study often became frustrated by how little the staff paid attention to parents' own expertise – as this parent relates:

> **Parent 1:** You see, in my experience I warned them ... I knew what was coming and, you wait, as soon as he starts getting a bit older, he is going to go violent on you because you are not understanding, you are not understanding where he is going, and

he is getting frustrated. He is trying to communicate with you and I'm trying to help you. I am printing you off the stuff and I am bringing you the stuff to school to try and get people to understand him. You know, I am going into school on a regular basis ... I am there and I am helping and it's not working, and by the end of Year 2 he is, like, throwing chairs at people and carving up tables, and here we go again.

Parent 2: And they just see you as some irate mother, they just see you as ...

Parent 1: .. like you are overprotective.

Broomhead (2013) found that parents with children whose SEND presented as challenging behaviour felt a greater sense of guilt and blame from educational professionals than parents whose child's SEND was related to a social communication need. In her study, Broomhead suggests that these emotions lead to parents seeking out labels to attribute blame elsewhere and reduce their own guilt. These feelings may be attributable to societal norms and expectations within different education systems:

Parent 1: ...when they're little, their behaviour can sometimes be the same as everybody else's, when they are in infants. Teachers are just dealing with another child that has just wet themselves, or just tripped up, or lost a coat or whatever, and everybody is quite calm. It is expected, it is going to happen. As they start getting to Year 9 and 10, well, they shouldn't be doing that now. But your child is ... I have got more problems now she is 13 than I did when she was 4.

Parent 2: Oh, definitely.

As a child with SEND moves through the education system, expectations and norm values shift, as does the level of nurturing provided. This position is based on adult-driven agendas to serve a system that is designed to fit a particular political position and comply with what is perceived as valuable in meeting societal needs. Consequently, needs can go unmet, not simply because of resource distribution, but also because of embedded cultural norms and values. It seems reasonable that parents consequently fail to feel confident about the abilities of teaching staff to meet their child's need:

Parent: I think a lot of it is to do with confidence of teachers, which has to do with skilling, which has to do with training ...

a teacher has to be confident to be able to say, actually, this is bigger than we can deal with. A lot of the time they are just doing their best ...

Although this parent believes that the teachers' confidence that they can meet children's SEND requirements is inadequate, possibly because of their initial training, we must also consider factors such as the prioritization of SEND in ITT curricula, the value placed by society on children and young people who have SEND, and the cultural norms that govern that society and localized contexts. Parents may well, at a meta-level at least, have low expectations of the education system meeting the needs of their child. This is a central challenge made by SRV theorists (for example, Wolfensberger, 1995), and must be systematically addressed in order to improve long-term outcomes for those with SEND (for example, Osburn, 1998, 2006; Race *et al.*, 2005), alongside improved SEND training for staff in mainstream education settings (Mann *et al.*, 2016).

We acknowledge that many schools can and do provide an appropriate level of support for children with SEND and their families. Often, it is the simple actions that make all the difference:

SENDCo: ... a particular child has come to school from nursery with an identified need, and concerns from parents and the nursery. [We are] now looking at the child in Reception [class], so are continuing to look at whether now he is in a different environment whether those needs are less apparent or more apparent. I would look at the bigger picture of any medical reports that have come through; I would probably also start off with some sort of family support process as well, just to make sure that all the information was round a table and that we had got all information from different sides ... so I think there will be so many different questions.

The SENDCo here describes how she intends to monitor and adjust input for a child transitioning from nursery with an identified SEND. Identifying appropriate informal SEND and family support processes and working within SEND guidance, equating to a graduated response, is exactly the response that best supports most children with suspected, emerging and identified SEND. In this case, that included good communication between parents, nursery and school, as well as an externally facilitated transition plan. Surely this supports the development of trusting relationships and confidence between parents and school, reducing the need for formal SEND processes and improving outcomes for the children:

> **Parent:** Well, I think as a parent when you come across that, you are so relieved and it is an emotional experience to come across somebody who does their job sensibly and grasps what the point of all this is. It is not something to do with not getting sued themselves, it is to do with helping the child, and that is what you are interested in and that's what your child is interested in. If they are interested in that as well, then that is a glorious thing.

However, this kind of inclusive practice should be circular, whether formal SEND processes become necessary or not. Rather, in some cases, having a Plan can, perceptually at least, be considered an end point, which may lead to relinquished responsibility. For example, the maintenance of a Plan becomes the responsibility of the local authority, the child may be placed within another setting or considered as having certified, within-child deficits, that are unresponsive to good-quality inclusive practice. PCRs can be used as a way of maintaining inclusive practice, using any Plan as a guiding tool for short-term action plans.

The needs of those initiating SEND processes

So far, we have discussed how parents, school staff and support professionals experience formal and informal SEND processes. We now consider the emotional, relational and practical needs for those initiating SEND processes.

Affective responses

> **Parent:** … when you have a child [with SEND], to get that [formal plan], you spend all your time telling everybody how bad the situation is, how awful they are, what their disabilities are, what they can and cannot do. Every other parent with a standard, average, child is gloating about their child and how wonderful they are and have got their GCSEs and all the rest of it. To get your [formal plan], and to get your help and support that you need, you have to make it look it pretty black, and that is how you spend your entire life …

Children with SEND make significant emotional demands on their parents. The rhetoric of parents tends to focus on their high levels of anxiety and concern that their child's needs are not being met, and their overwhelming feelings that they have to fight the school system:

Parent 1: Well, the problem I have got is, from what I have heard, I have not got a cat in hell's chance [of getting an EHCP], but I cannot see any other way of beating the system.

Parent 2: You've got to have one.

Parent 3: For me, I felt like if I had one then perhaps my request for extra understanding for him, and extra attention for him, would have been taken more seriously.

Initial frustration and lack of confidence in the school translates, directly in this case, into a parent requesting a formal SEND assessment. There appears to be no evidence of whether or not the child's needs could or should be met within their setting. The parent's request appears to provide some containment and, if a Plan is agreed, some reassurance that their child's needs will be met:

CP: I think the parents feel that an EHCP would give them confidence that schools are definitely going to do those things. Whereas I think that sometimes that's not always the case. I think, quite often, a lot of things could be put in place anyway, and without it needing to go through EHCP, but I think parents feel very worried if they don't get the EHCP and think that those things aren't going to be put in place.

It is almost inevitable that parents feel a strong drive to protect the needs of their child. In the context we have outlined, parents do not see a skilled workforce, and observe inherent cultural devaluing of those with SEND. However, such an individualistic perspective overlooks the importance of the collective, and places inordinate pressure upon services so that the demands become unmanageable. This position gives parents reasons to advocate for their child with intense emotion. We believe such emotion may be unconscious, but it nevertheless contributes to the high demand for formal SEND processes. Inevitably, inequalities emerge between the children of parents who have the means to take on the system and those who do not:

Parent: ... I went right up to tribunal for [child's name], and we spent a lot of money on a specialist solicitor to get there and, yes, ended up brokering a deal the day before tribunal. Yes, a bit of a bittersweet process really, because we got what we wanted for our daughter but I thought the process was just so flawed it was untrue. The fact that [the local authority] has to spend money on legal teams to go to tribunals, and it could be better spent.

This parent, quite legitimately, proceeded to appeal an original decision made in relation to a formal SEND assessment for her daughter, spurred on by the distress the process caused her. She was, however, able to challenge the local authority by means of prerequisite conditions – such as having access to resources. Others may challenge by other means, such as by writing to their MP. Again, this requires certain basic conditions, such as being literate, articulate and knowledgeable about the system, and in some cases access to, or the resources to raise, funds. But even when parents do have the necessary skills and resources, they are not well placed to advocate, simply because they are the parents:

> **Parent:** I should be able to do this stuff, but it is very difficult to do it for your own children because you can't. You know you want to be very involved, but it is hard, you know. I could do it for somebody else, I could have been that woman for somebody else. I could have sat there and said to someone – you must have something in about this. I found it very hard to do it for myself because it feels like, I don't know, it is difficult enough to have distance on the child … it is difficult to always see the worst case all the time, as you live your life always trying to see the best case and trying to be positive.

The differences in skills, knowledge and resources leave space for individualistic perspectives to create inequalities between children. Although the local authority must use due diligence to make rational decisions about how to use limited resources based on case-by-case evidence, the parents who do have the resources, knowledge and skills are in a privileged position to mount a challenge. This is not to suggest, in any way, that parents should not advocate for their child, but rather to highlight the inequalities that are created. And this raises an ethical issue for service providers when considering how to equalize access to services. For example, a parent who is able to articulate their concerns to their local MP, who is then in a position to lobby service managers, should not be at any greater advantage than a parent who is not so placed:

> **Interviewer:** … what led you to consider or request your statutory assessment over, or in addition to, what is already available outside of the process, such as the local offer, in school intervention or external agency support?

> **Parent:** I feel like, if it is outside of school or whatever, I can totally coordinate that – I am fine being captain of my ship … I'm well in with my own responsibilities for my own kids. When it is in school … I'm not sure who's doing what and what is supposed to be happening, and who knows what and who doesn't know stuff, and why is this happening that way …

One frustration voiced by teachers we spoke to is that a child is one of hundreds in school, and that parents' expectations seem not to take this into account. What staff might want to deliver may be impossible among competing demands and needs. Liberalism is a philosophical school of thought that sees the separation of the individual from society – there is a shift from focusing on the we towards focusing on the I, for example asking, 'am I and my family OK?', as opposed to 'are we and our community OK?' This philosophy has found its way into political rhetoric and has steadily become embedded in cultural norm values (Augoustinos *et al.,* 2014). In recent history, this is most notable in, although not exclusive to, Thatcherism. Margaret Thatcher was Prime Minister of Britain from 1979 to 1990. To her, there was no society, only individuals who must prioritize and resolve their own difficulties:

> I think we have gone through a period when too many children and people have been given to understand 'I have a problem, it is the Government's job to cope with it!' or 'I have a problem, I will go and get a grant to cope with it!' 'I am homeless, the Government must house me!' and so they are casting their problems on society and who is society? There is no such thing! There are individual men and women and there are families and no government can do anything except through people and people look to themselves first. (Thatcher, 1987)

Thatcher's views had a pronounced impact on the collective perspective of society that can engage in group action. Individualism found its way into popular culture, epitomized by the comedian Harry Enfield's character, Loadsamoney. Such views exacerbated inequality in the distribution of wealth, dividing the haves and the have-nots. We see a resurgence of this pattern today (Corlett and Clarke, 2017). However, it would be misleading to believe that parents do not take responsibility for their children or are not aware of the pressures that schools face. In fact, our study found that parents often went well beyond what one might reasonably expect:

Parent: If you counted up all the hours you had done, what you had to do that [school] should have been doing – it's thousands. I mean, it's absolutely wrecked me; I'm ill, I'm unwell, I can't work anymore – it has frazzled my brain, I've got fibromyalgia; it's the stress of it all.

Paradoxically, the inadequate support that the parents we spoke to felt they were offered only led to greater pressure on social systems and reduced the labour market. It would be wrong to attribute individualistic perspectives to parents. Rather, it is a social and cultural issue about which practitioners should be aware when planning to meet the needs of children with SEND while providing containment for parents who, quite legitimately, feel a great deal of angst:

Parent 1: ... you know that child is going to go into the school and you know that they will sink, [be] picked on, bullied. I was going to have more mental health problems than I already had, if she put one foot over the threshold in that high school.

Parent 2: I have seen over and over again with friends, there is no point in persisting with a school that doesn't get it; you just get out.

Parents are distressed if schools fail to meet their child's SEND requirements. In this case, the parent had lost all confidence in the school staff, causing her to remove her child. And it may not end there: the child may end up being home educated or schooled outside their local community.

Support-seeking behaviour

The rationale of those requesting access to formal SEND processes was also linked to seeking support, typically from external, specialist services such as educational psychologists. This might relate to appropriate one-to-one support for health and safety reasons, or accessing a complex needs setting as here:

Head: Yes, presently, we have only got two children in school with a Statement, one has a very severe physical need and therefore the Statement has provided us with the absolute security, I guess, of knowing that we can have one-to-one support for that child ... without that, the child couldn't be in a mainstream school, and it is the parents' absolute wish that that child is in a mainstream school.

However, often support being sought was already available within informal SEND support structures, such as the local offer, a graduated response, or preventative intervention:

> **EHCPCo:** ... when it has been those children that are suddenly causing schools, you know, that are destroying classrooms and aggressive behaviour to other children, it is a kind of timescale seems to be too long. [Schools] do permanently exclude and will say that they cannot [keep] this child in mainstream school, they are going to need a Plan and specialist provision. But a lot of those sort of issues are very much around social and behavioural issues at home ...

We found cases where formal SEND processes were instigated, either to deal with a crisis or as a response to the family's difficulties in supporting the child. However, many schools work conscientiously to identify gaps in the provision they are able to access, and only request formal SEND support where it is appropriate:

> **DH:** ... if [the needs are] manageable within school and what we have got in school [and] the child's needs aren't over and above what we could already give them without bringing in some kind of specialism.

A number of changes in recent years have had an impact on how SEND is managed. For example, academization has devolved power away from local authorities to schools, and budgets are now provided directly to schools, in place of the centrally maintained specialist services, which were free at the point of delivery:

> **EP:** ... schools are expected to be much more mature organizations, businesslike organizations, and have experience of SEN alongside other things, and I'm not so convinced how much guidance, how much training, has been put in [to] schools in order [for them] to function as mature organizations in those aspects of SEN ...

Thus, there are likely to be significant differences and inequalities between communities in the way in which available resources are used. Local authorities do retain a budget to manage statutory SEND demands, such as formal assessment. As the psychologist below observes, these issues could lead to schools seeking support services that might otherwise be met within their own resources:

EP: ... in the past, people would say use our service. Going way back, we used to have behaviour support assistants who would go into schools and support, and there was also school-to-school ... a lot of things have changed because since the statutory process we have gone through a massive change in local authorities and how services are delivered and commissioned, and I think the very fact that schools don't now get equal support in resources, makes them often more panicky. Not every school [here] has an EP, that's one thing, so that's going to make a lot of difference ... some haven't bought into that.

How services are systemically set up, and the impact of national reforms, could exacerbate the perceived need of support services being accessed via other means, and thus push up requests for formal SEND processes. These systemic challenges are seen in other areas of the Code of Practice too. A key part of the SEND reforms in England and Wales has been the extension of provision for young people aged 19 to 25:

Parent: ... some young people have that input from all the sources from an early age, but just because they are not there by a certain age, it doesn't mean to say there is not a need for them. I think there are weaknesses in the systems, certainly on the health side when you move from Children's Services into Adult Services, particularly around the mental health area; they need to be very clearly identified. I certainly think there is a case for saying all young people should have somebody representing all areas [of need] at that age of around 17 or 18, to ensure that as we go forward into adulthood the right strands are being looked at.

One reason for this extension was to ensure a smooth transition between adult and children's services, so providing valuable onward support for the young person, even though, as we have seen, a Plan does not necessarily lead to greater multi-agency working or professional engagement. Furthermore, an EHCP is likely to be ceased by a local authority when the young person is over 18 and no longer in education or training, or if they begin attending a higher education course (DfE/DoH, 2015). This may not be helpful for those who may be among the most at risk of harm.

Some years ago I (Nick) worked in an inner-city area of the UK. One day, I visited a youth court, where a 17-year-old female, who had been arrested for a relatively petty criminal offence, sat before the magistrates. It transpired that this young woman had an extensive criminal record and had found herself in a spiralling state of drug use and prostitution. She was given a custodial sentence, the magistrates noting in their summing up that this was for her own protection. They said it was the only way they could be sure she would access the support they believed she needed.

This case has stuck with me for years. Are custodial sentences and criminal records the only way we can secure the protection of our most at-risk groups of young people? A young person does not typically reach crisis point without an extensive and complex history. It made me wonder what this young woman's journey had been. The Children and Families Act 2014 offered some hope for such young people – a Plan that would bring together education, health and social care – yet, if she was unwilling or unable to access education, there would be no such support. This raises the questions of how far a Plan legitimately helps coordinate health and social care services and of who advocates for the child when there is no parent or guardian to fulfil that role with the rigour we have seen from the parents who contributed to our study.

Quality of communication

We know that a key driver in requesting formal SEND processes is to access additional resources or support. However, poor understanding of what is available within formal and informal SEND processes is an endemic problem, which creates a great deal of confusion, anxiety and misuse of both sets of procedures:

> **EP:** I think there is something really important here, which is that there are two processes working together. People's understanding of … what's available and getting rid of that notion that the authority supplies. At the same time, we have got a new Act, which has made significant changes to the way we work with children with special needs. The two things need to be fitted together, schools haven't yet married the two together. Until schools are clear about how they can use their resources most effectively and work together to get the best for their children in their clusters, we will have this growing EHCP requests until something changes.

As we noted, a contributing factor is the notion of a personal budget and the sense that there is additional funding available for those with an EHCP:

> **DH:** My understanding is that there is a pot of money tied in that the parents can drive, or schools, and that ties in together. That is my understanding of it at this moment in time.

Interviewer: Because of the personal budget?

DH: Yes.

Although there is some flexibility, and therefore variability, across England and Wales over how personal budgets are managed, current local practice is that these funds are effectively taken from funding that has already been delegated to clusters of schools. So, unless there is a very high level of need, such as the necessity to change a building layout or facility – for example, for a wheelchair ramp or shower cubicle – a personal budget would come from funding already available within the cluster of schools. Thus, the same pot of money is already available without the need for formal SEND processes. The confusion at the systems level also filters down to affect how parents understand what is available to their child. As this psychologist highlights, clarity in this respect is greatly needed so as to manage expectations of parents more sensitively:

> **EP 1:** We need to be clear, so that schools are clear what is out there, so parents are clear what's available. We talked about the local offer, not many people, even professionals who are working through the EHCP process, are clear about the local offer and how to use it effectively. You know that young people probably can't access that, so there are so many things that need to be sorted out for us and ...
>
> **EP 2:** Yes. Clarity, yes.

Yet we still see very poor understanding of how informal SEND resources, such as those available through the local offer, can be utilized. Importantly, parents are calling for transparency in the messages being given, so their expectations can be managed:

> **Parent:** ... even if the system has to turn around and say we cannot afford to fund that – that's the problem, nobody will be honest. In a commercial environment, it has to be out on the line, you know, the figures are talked about and projects happen or don't happen based on whether or not there is the right resourcing going into them. I know you cannot take a person in quite the same sort of way, but [just] turn around and say, sorry parent's income is beyond a certain level, that means we can't afford it. I think that's the way forward ... at least as a parent knows that's the way, you know, the way it's got to be done ... I think there needs to be a bit more upfrontness about all of this, as otherwise parents do

end up waiting for the system to provide it, and when it doesn't you end up with the difficult situations and upset parents and you know.

Even when SEND processes have been initiated, and parents are clear on what to expect, their experiences of professional advice around a child's SEND are not always helpful:

> **Parent:** ... I don't know if anyone else has experienced this, but can we have an EP report that actually says something and means something to a parent.
>
> **Interviewer:** Tell me more ...
>
> **Parent:** ... well, I have had one for my son, and I read through it and thought, what's that telling me? There are lots of you know, zeros on this scale and that scale, and I thought this doesn't say what that means.

But not all parents felt that information about their child's needs was poorly communicated:

> **Parent 1:** I thought I understood my EP's report.
>
> **Parent 2:** Yes, I did ...
>
> **Parent 3:** I didn't understand my private one because it had all the jargon in it; it was, you know, not in English.

This raises useful points over individual practice styles and whether different parents find professional reports more or less accessible. Professional views must be clearly communicated. PCRs can be an effective way not only of communicating, but also of co-constructing the nature of a child's SEND collaboratively, as we discuss in Chapter 3.

Quality of relationships

> **Parent:** ... they have not just wrecked my son's life, they have wrecked my life, and because my older kids don't understand it they cannot get on with him. They have wrecked the family relationship; everything is wrecked. Because they just couldn't do what they were supposed to do – educate your child.

Good relationships between parents, schools, local authorities and support professionals are essential to promoting positive outcomes for children and young people. The parents we spoke to found all forms of SEND processes stressful when they did not feel supported by the wider system or the professionals. This appears to have a significant impact on the family, making parents feel isolated:

> **Parent:** There is such an air of, like, struggle and distrust and ... in all of this, really, relationships, in trying to speak to all these people in school and trying to speak to the specialist, and trying to get stuff done for your kid, you know.

Positive relationships between parents and schools are crucial. As this psychologist reflects, poor relationships can undermine the parent's confidence that the staff are meeting their child's specific needs, and provoke them to request a formal SEND process:

> **CP:** I think it is about looking at, and I think that's when that good relationship with the school comes in, where the school feels able to put that support in place. It is a key thing is transitioning, into assembly, say, that they know at that time they need the existing support in the classroom to really focus in on that child. Then I think that is fine. I think if the school feels less able to do that, then it is about making the statutory kind of guidance saying this is what this child needs and they need, because otherwise they are never going to get into an assembly and they are never going to have that learning opportunity.

We saw that the approach taken by school staff can depend on the age of the child and the consequent expectations set by the education system. Here, a parent describes how she was happy with the school's provision and her relationship with the staff at first, but how this changed over time:

> **Parent:** ... one of my children has congenital hemiplegia, but she is quite independent. She started with Portage [a service for pre-school children with SEND and their families, usually offered in the form of home visits], so had loads of therapy and is pretty functional, but she does require help here and there and a little bit of extra time here and there for stuff sometimes. She cannot carry her tray at lunchtime and in the beginning the school was quite helpful and we didn't, I didn't feel like we needed any kind of a [formal SEND process] or anything like that. I feel we were just kind of getting along, and the school were being kind and understanding and it was obvious what was wrong with her. As time has gone by, there have been a few incidents already

> where she has come home crying because she has been in trouble because she has taken so long to do something or she can't do something. She has not eaten because she has dropped her tray at lunch, whereas before she had a teacher to help her with lunch ...

Often, small adjustments can be enough to improve a parent's confidence in, and relationship with, staff. It is helpful to have a link person between school and parents – be it a class teacher, teaching assistant or member of pastoral support staff – who is able to spend a little time building this relationship:

> **Parent:** ... for me, just having things written down on paper – who is responsible for stuff, who is supposed to know about stuff, who do I go to if the kid comes home and starts telling me stuff that's happened during the day. Obviously, I'm not there to see it, so who do I contact when stuff like that is going on, who is going to be my friend in all of this? Who's going to be my kid's friend in all this?

However, every child is likely to be one of hundreds in a school. So, individualizing support in this way may not always be possible – even if it is expected. This creates a particular difficulty that requires resolving at local level, possibly by adopting effective personalized approaches, such as PCRs. Importantly, though, some schools put in a lot of effort to sustain positive relationships with parents:

> **Parent:** [My daughter is] going back to school, this time she is really struggling; she has quite a lot of problems that are impacting on her and other children. [The school] have reeled in their ASD unit support worker to start work with her, and ... I had the teacher on the phone last night for 45 minutes at 7 p.m. going through everything. She said she would phone us up and she has; the way she is trying to deal with it is absolutely fantastic, and they are trying to share it with us. Everything gets printed out and laminated in words, figures, pictures, symbols, and they are just looking after her.

This degree of care is akin to the expectations held of teachers in Norway. But, as we saw in this comparative example, for an approach to be widespread, it must be filtered down from the policymakers. The Code of Practice (DfE/DoH, 2015) does allow provision of a caseworker who can support the parents through the formal SEND process. As this parent relates, having access to this caseworker, particularly where relationships with school are fractured, was very reassuring:

> **Parent:** High school were not interested in transfer at all. I had the rudest – I even came here and complained about it – the rudest member of staff in the high school. At that point, I pulled out and said, that's it, she's not going up, I am going to home educate. That was the first time my caseworker spoke to me, when I sent that email through, and within three minutes she was on the phone.

This scenario is peppered with reactive action that might not be in the best interests of the child. Initially, the school did not instigate a transition plan with which the parents were satisfied. This led to the child's withdrawal into home education, which could create serious challenges for the family and for the child's progress. Only then did the assigned caseworker contact parents following a complaint. If such situations can be managed proactively, a great deal of stress could be saved, and a more family-centred approach to meeting need could be maintained. If parents feel contained, trust can be fostered, which will have a resounding favourable impact on the child:

> **Parent 1:** It is that whole issue of trust again, isn't it; there are so many things that have gone wrong with, like, communication, just like there is no trust and the kids, my kids at least, don't trust ...
>
> **Parent 2:** ... my son doesn't trust ...

In this chapter, we have explored the experiences of parents, support professionals and school staff of the formal and informal SEND processes in England and Wales. We identified the key rationales for why different SEND processes might be initiated, in light of the emotional, support-seeking, communicative and relational issues. Our findings form the basis on which we developed a personalized approach to meeting the needs of children in the shape of PCRs. In Chapter 3, we provide a practical guide to how to establish PCRs in settings, based on empirical findings from Cycle 2 of our study.

Chapter 3

Preparing for a PCR

> *Everyone is different, it's the natural state.*
> *It's the facts, it's plain to see,*
> *The world's grey enough without making it worse.*
> *What we need is individuality.*
> Lee Hall and Elton John, 'Expressing yourself' (2005)

This chapter presents two case examples that explain how our PCR model worked. We combine critical theory with evidence from our research participants to create the stories of John and Katie, who each have SEND, and their families. We explore the PCR process, and outline the practicalities of setting up and running it. We also share the resources we developed as part of our research, presenting storyboards, a child-friendly report template and other visual materials.

Case examples

John attends a mainstream secondary school and has a diagnosis of autism. He has a keen interest in trains and enjoys sophisticated logic-based board games. John is considering options for his future and his parents are becoming increasingly concerned about preparing him for independent living in the long term. A PCR was a way of bringing key people together to ensure John's needs were being met and to begin thinking about his future.

Katie is a primary-age child who struggles to regulate her emotions, and this is affecting her learning. The school SENDCo has tried a range of strategies and intervention groups with Katie, but these have had limited impact. School staff and Katie's mother are keen to understand how best to support her. Katie's mother and the school SENDCo had recently considered requesting an EHCP. We suggested that a PCR would be a way of formalizing the graduated assess–plan–do–review cycle, and would identify any additional support needed and allow progress to be monitored over time.

Summary of the PCR process

Katie and John both experienced the same basic PCR structure:

1. **Preparation:** Katie and John each took part in pre-meeting activities to gather their views on their situations. We told them, and the adults

involved, what they could expect of a PCR, using the visual resources set out below.

2. **Arrival:** John and Katie each entered a room in their school, along with their parents and familiar school staff, including the SENDCo, key worker and, in Katie's case, the head teacher. The facilitator, an educational psychologist, introduced himself and explained what would happen during the PCR. Particular attention was given to how a PCR differed from traditional meetings. The facilitator then introduced the ground rules.

3. **Sign-in:** At each meeting, Katie and John chose a coloured pen for themselves, followed by the adults. (Do not include a yellow pen in the choice, as it might not show up clearly in photographs.) The facilitator always uses the black pen, the neutral colour. Each person used their own coloured pen to record their views on the sheets of paper hung around the room. Everyone present then signed in on the first sheet of paper with their own pen.

4. **Answering the questions:** Everyone was then invited to write or draw their answers to each question on the sheets hung around the room. The SENDCo, who had completed the activities with them earlier, helped John and Katie, although both thought of new things they wanted to say and recorded these views too. In both cases, this part of the process took about 15 minutes.

5. **Summarizing:** After everyone had recorded their views, the facilitator asked everyone to come back together. He summarized what everyone had written, occasionally seeking to clarify a comment or word someone had used. Both John and Katie returned to their classrooms after the affirmative parts of the summary were completed – that is, addressing the questions about what we admire and what is working well for the child.

6. **Action plan:** The facilitator then used the content of the session to tease out ideas about what might be happening in the young person's situation. This evoked ideas about further assessments and interventions that might be helpful, and the adults drew up a live action plan. Then John and Katie were each invited back to listen to the outline of the action plan, and were offered the opportunity to add to, change or question any part of the plan, and ultimately give it their seal of approval.

We now consider each element of the PCR procedure from different perspectives.

Preparing for a PCR

The SENDCos for both Katie and John felt that PCRs were an efficient use of time because they led to clear, co-produced action plans that identified, met and supported the needs of the children concerned:

> **SENDCo:** … [PCRs are] far more time efficient … I mean, for me, what I have had to put in the past with paper-led exercises, you spend ages and it is backwards and forwards. This was kind of almost done in one hit, if you like.

> **SENDCo:** It felt like we achieved something in a short space of time; it's positive … it was nice having the parents and children and professionals there – it was holistic around the child.

The first SENDCo observed that paper-led exercises, such as EHCP requests, are extremely time-consuming and often challenging to put together, whereas PCRs are fast, effective and, as the second SENDCo describes, can bring together a team around the child. However, the SENDCo in Katie's case found it difficult to convince others to move away from assessment towards a consultative model of working:

> **SENDCo (Katie):** … it took a lot of preparation behind the scenes, explaining what it meant and why it was a good way to be doing things, and how it met the Code of Practice … it took a bit of convincing for some people that it was going to be a better way of doing things than the old-fashioned assessment model.

Staff found that it took time to establish PCRs as a legitimate alternative to previous ways of working. Both John's and Katie's PCRs took considerable investment in time initially, particularly as this was a new way of working for their schools. However, once both head teachers saw the benefits of the PCRs, the initial investment became justified.

General principles of preparing for a PCR

As far as possible, PCRs should be organized alongside the focus person. However, when working with children and certain SEND, it is necessary to work collaboratively with adults who know the child well and with those skilled in eliciting the views of the child, such as psychologists or social workers. Katie's and John's SENDCos had both used the activities in this book to elicit their views before the meeting. When preparing for John's and Katie's PCRs, we used the following approach:

- We identified that Katie and John would benefit from a PCR based on a case outline we provided earlier. The SENDCos worked with the children to ensure they understood what a PCR is and what is involved. The SENDCos watched the short film we created as part of this research to help explain the process:

  www.youtube.com/watch?v=aWjjXsu6MY8

- We identified an appropriate time and date for the PCRs to take place. In both cases, this was a quiet space in school. However, when working with children, particularly in school, one should consider factors, such as which lesson the child might be removed from to attend, and whether the meeting will run over a break or lunchtime.
- Both Katie and John were attending school, so this was a convenient venue for the PCR. But if, for example, a child is refusing school or is unhappy there, a neutral space is desirable, such as the children's centre or in the focus person's home.
- During the elicitation activities, the school's SENDCo for both John and Katie asked them who they might like to invite to their meeting. Although not relevant to either Katie's or John's case, safeguarding issues should always be considered. It may be necessary to invite some people and not possible to invite others because there are safeguarding concerns. In such cases, the child should be told before they are asked who they would like to invite, thus ensuring that safe, adult boundaries are in place.

The room has to have enough space to hang seven large sheets of paper from the walls, and for the people at the meeting to move around comfortably:

> EP: ... it was a large room, so even though there were half a dozen if not seven people wandering around the room writing ... I felt that it was a good process. If the room had been smaller and the wall space had been cluttered, I think it would possibly have been a less positive experience, so I think when you are arranging meetings like this, you do have to have regard to the practicalities because it is a bit like anything, good preparation makes it seem effortless.

Choose the space accordingly, while also taking into account the child's familiarity with the location. Sanderson and Lewis (2012) suggest that meetings can usefully be held in the focus person's home or another space they select, although we have found this difficult to organize or rather inappropriate. What matters is how the child will feel, as Katie's deputy head says:

> **DH:** ... we had quite an intimate room, it wasn't that big [but] it was a very child-centred room, so Katie felt very relaxed in the environment. She had been into the environment beforehand ... if you have got a blank room, it can look, I guess, quite clinical, whereas we had deliberately chosen an area which was very child-friendly.

With academization, many schools have complete financial control, and so have to be more businesslike in their decisions, as school budgets have recently been cut. This has its challenges: the financial implications of any recommendations drawn from a PCR should be discussed with the commissioner of the work, such as the head teacher, in advance of the PCR. This was certainly true in Katie's case, as her SENDCo explains:

> **SENDCo:** So, actually, as we have got to know the process more, we know that sometimes, it is going to lead to another piece of work being offered and we [me and the head] should have just had that professional conversation before ... can we afford it? And they are really tough decisions for professionals to make in this climate, because you want to be there helping every single child with exactly what they need, but the truth is we prioritize.

Given the nature of the meeting, and some of the challenges that might emerge through the discussions, PCRs can become uncomfortable. Awkward moments must be managed with care, and respect must be shown to everyone involved. Sometimes, one can alert schools beforehand to the issues that might arise, but in many cases this will not be possible, so the wording used on the action plan should allow for post-meeting reflections; for example:

- the head teacher will consider X assessment and contact Y for further discussion
- the SENDCo will contact X professional to discuss possible referral
- the SENDCo will make an application for funding from X.

This phrasing still emphasizes the actions that are required and the tasks that are to be brought back to the review meeting for discussion, but it also provides professional space to make informed and measured decisions, away from the pressure of a public forum. Although these actions might cause further delay, we found that in the cases of both Katie and John this expedited action from those involved while maintaining constructive relationships. We discuss facilitation skills a little later.

Preparing children

In the cases of both Katie and John, their school, their parents and the other support professionals involved were sent a pack of information in order to prepare the children and everyone involved for the PCR. This is a vital part of the PCR process. The packs included materials to help everyone, including the child, to better understand what a PCR is and what will happen in the run-up and during the process. Figure 3.1 is an artist's impression of a PCR meeting, showing four key points that one might expect.

1. You may have noticed large sheets of paper hanging on the walls. Everyone will get the chance to get up and write or draw their responses to the different questions displayed on these sheets of paper.

2. There will be enough space to move around – we never sit too long in a PCR!

3. A visitor from outside your school will help run your meeting. This person is called a facilitator. The facilitator is super friendly and is there to support everyone.

4. The room will be set up so everyone feels comfortable. Everyone in the room will be there to support you and your family.

Figure 3.1: PCR meeting – discussion mat

The SENDCos in John's and Katie's schools used this discussion mat flexibly. Katie was much younger, so for her it was used as a storyboard. This was later extended by using it alongside the storyboard provided in Figure 3.2. This is an artist's impression of what happens leading up to and in a PCR. Because John was older, his SENDCo gave him the discussion mat in advance so he could read it and discuss anything he found unclear or worrying.

1. Before your PCR a teacher from school will meet with you to gather your views. They will ask questions like what is going well and what you might like more help with.

2. At the start of your meeting the facilitator will introduce ground rules. These 'rules' are there to help everyone feel safe and supported.

3. Next, everyone takes a different coloured pen and is asked to write or draw their answers to questions displayed on large sheets of paper.

4. Once finished, the facilitator uses the sheets of paper to help everyone come up with an action plan of how we will help you reach your goals.

Figure 3.2: PCR process storyboard

The discussion mat and storyboard were used in conjunction with the child-friendly film. Staff of the setting and the child's parents used these tools with John and Katie to help everyone feel prepared for the PCR. Katie and John each met their SENDCos to gather their views for sharing at the meetings. Eliciting the views of children in advance does not preclude them from stating their views during the PCR meeting. Rather, the preliminary meeting gives the child the opportunity to be further prepared by knowing what the questions will be and having pre-populated activity sheets that they can use as an aide-memoire in the PCR meeting. As this psychologist found, pre-elicitation became an essential part of the process:

> **EP:** ... thinking about children being able to communicate their views, I don't know how it would work if they weren't particularly verbal, so if they had communication difficulties or if they were non-verbal, if it would mean a member of staff signing, [and] they would then translate that on to the bits of paper; I'm not too sure how it would work if a child didn't have very good verbal or language skills.

Initially, we used pre-existing elicitation activities, such as those set out in Sanderson and Lewis (2012). Although these resources are good, and helpful for adults and older children such as John, they did not fit into our

PCR meetings more generally. Younger children such as Katie struggled to access these activities, so we set out to develop new resources that combined new ideas with existing approaches that are designed to support all young people to share their views (see Clark and Moss, 2011).

Both SENDCos were given the following activities, and asked to assign a PCR champion. This will be a class teacher, key worker or the SENDCo himself or herself. In both Katie's and John's cases, the school SENDCos took on the role of PCR champion. The PCR champion works with the child to prepare them for the meeting and complete the elicitation activities. During the meeting, the PCR champion helps the child record their views on the sheets of paper.

Preparation activities

The following activities were used with both Katie and John, but they may not be suitable for all children. Rather, activities are chosen according to factors such as developmental stage, presenting needs and language ability. Each activity fits one of the six questions that will be displayed on the day:

1. What do you admire about X?
2. What is going well for X?
3. What is not working well for X?
4. What is important to X now?
5. What might be important to X in the next 6 to 12 months?
6. Are there any questions you would like answered?

Both SENDCos were asked to complete at least one activity for each question. Here we use the preparation activities used by Katie's SENDCo as a working example. The initial activity is designed to be a simple icebreaker, and to gather some basic information from the child (see Box 1).

BOX 1: ICEBREAKER AND INFORMATION-GATHERING ACTIVITY

All about me

My name is _____. I am ___ years old.

I live in _____ with _____.

My best friend is _____.

My favourite activity is _____.

At school I really like _____.

I get help from _____.

I don't like _____.

At home I really like _____.

I can get help from _____.

I don't like _____.

Activities for Question 1

The first set of activities links to the question '*What do you admire about Katie?*' They were designed to understand how Katie viewed herself.

Self-esteem piggy bank: We gave Katie a picture of a piggy bank and asked her to think about things that make her feel good. We gave examples such as activities or lessons she is good at, the people in her life she is close to, and the positive attributes she identifies with, such as 'I am kind'. These ideas were written onto post-it notes with the SENDCo's help, and Katie stuck them on the piggy bank.

Like many other children, Katie found this task a little tricky – it can be difficult to think of things we like about ourselves. Certain questions can help: 'what would your teacher say you are good at?' Or, 'what would your friend say is the best thing about you?' It is useful for the PCR champion to know the child well. Katie's SENDCo knew her well, and so could suggest some ideas about what they admire, although this should be avoided if possible. The SENDCo did make it clear which were her suggestions and which were Katie's. Where an idea originated from the SENDCo, she further indicated whether Katie agreed with her or not. This meant we could all be clear which of the views belonged to, or were endorsed by, Katie and which belonged to the adult working with her.

Projective questions: Katie then completed the projective questions task with the help of her PCR champion. Katie's task was to read aloud the following incomplete sentences, and complete them without thinking about it too much. Katie was allowed to review her answers at the end and change anything she was unhappy with:

I am good at _____.

I am at my best when _____.

My favourite hobby is _____.

I feel happiest when _____.

I like _____.

The best thing about me is _____.

I feel great when _____.

This activity is similar to the *all about me* questions, but aims to elicit more spontaneous, unfiltered answers about the child's strengths and interests. It can often feel more free-flowing as the child becomes less restricted by barriers such as doubt or self-criticism. Again, it may be suitable to scribe for the child, although Katie did not need this. Once the activity was completed, the SENDCo went through the questions and answers with Katie to ensure she was happy with the written account. From time to time this activity creates more discussion, which allows the child to expand on his or her initial responses, and recording this can add a greater depth to the responses.

Activities for Question 2

The second set of activities links to the question '*What is going well for Katie?*' These activities were designed to understand how Katie viewed her current level of support. Katie required a little support as the concepts became more abstract, with the SENDCo providing examples of who Katie might choose for each section. To reduce the risk of leading Katie to answer in a particular way, the SENDCo provided examples based on people she knew Katie would name, followed by the phrase 'is there anyone else who helps you at [context]?'. For example:

> **SENDCo:** Katie, we are going to think about people who support you in different places. First, let's think about home. I know your mum supports you at home, so we can put her name here, but is there anyone else who helps you are home?

Katie proceeded to list other people (and her pets) who help her at home in different ways.

Not all children will be aware of the support they are receiving. Nevertheless, the activities should be completed from the child's perspective – adults will have an opportunity to share their views during the PCR.

Circles of strength: Figure 3.3 is a template for this activity. The SENDCo first identified with Katie the people and support she receives from each of the four areas: home, school, friends, and activities and other support. Next, the SENDCo asked Katie in what ways each is important to her. For example, Katie's father, whom she identified in the 'home' box, helped her by reading a bedtime story and, in the 'school' box, a teaching assistant helped Katie with guided reading. However, it is important to remember that, as for all these activities, the focus is on what the child – not the adult – feels is helpful and supportive.

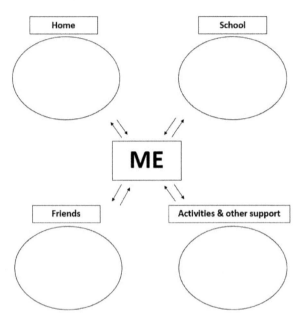

Figure 3.3: 'Circle of strength' activity: 'We are going to think about the people, activities and support that help you feel happy, safe and able to achieve'

The SENDCo also used an adapted version of the miracle question (for example, De Shazer and Dolan, 2012), which prompted Katie to produce a detailed version of what a perfect day would look and feel like for her. Within this lie clues to how to support the child.

Activities for Question 3

The third set of activities links to the question during the PCR '*What is not working well for Katie, what might you like to change?*' Here we are trying to identify future aspirations, the challenges or barriers that might stand in the way of achieving them, and ideas about how we might overcome such challenges or make things easier for Katie.

Three wishes: Katie was asked to imagine she had three wishes. She can wish for anything, except more wishes – a surprisingly common request! Some children struggle with this task, particularly younger children and those who have certain emotional or communication difficulties. In these cases, one can ask the child to think about something they would like to change at home or school. The discussion can then be expanded by asking them to consider how this change might come about, and whether anyone they know could help the wish come true. In Katie's case, she was able to complete the task without any additional support.

The SENDCo then used a version of what a typical bad day would look like (Sanderson and Lewis, 2012). This is the same as the miracle question used earlier, but in reverse. Katie's descriptions allowed adults to understand what barriers she might be experiencing, and thus find ways to work at easing or removing them.

Activities for Question 4

The fourth set of activities links to the question in the PCR '*What is important to Katie now?*' This section was aimed at understanding what Katie felt was important in her life right now. For Katie, this included the support she received in school, and friends, family members and hobbies, particularly horse riding. These activities also allow the PCR champion to identify the protective factors and strengths of the child, so they can be built on in the PCR.

Wall of important things: During this task, Katie was asked to draw or write what is really important to her at the moment: family, perhaps, or teachers, places, activities, lessons, support, hobbies or anything else she wished to share. Figure 3.4 is a template for gathering these views. Not all the spaces have to be filled, and additional spaces can be added if needed.

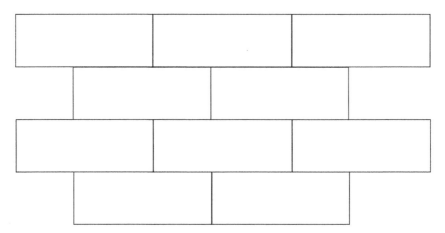

Figure 3.4: 'Wall of important things' activity

Desert island: In this task, Katie was free to draw or write her responses to the question: 'If you were going on a trip to a desert island, what three items would you take with you?' Her responses were expanded upon with support from the SENDCo. For example, Katie was asked why particular items were important and whether/how these things related to Katie's life now.

Activities for Question 5

The fifth set of activities links to the question '*What might be important to Katie in the next 6 to 12 months?*' Now we are seeking to identify what the short- to medium-term objectives are, according to Katie. These will be specific to the child, but could include upcoming transitions, such as moving school, learning a new skill or maintaining/improving a current skill, the support the child has access to and so on. Again, this task can be tricky for children with certain needs, such as those associated with autism, but Katie could answer without help. And, despite the nature of John's needs, he too could complete this task with only some example prompts to get him started.

The time machine: Katie was asked to imagine that she was going to step into a time machine, a bit like the one in the television series *Doctor Who*, and that she would be transported one year into the future. She was to begin thinking about things that would have changed in that time – for example, she was preparing to move year groups. In John's case, an upcoming move of school was the shared starting point. Once Katie had understood the task, the SENDCo explored what else she would like to see in the future by asking the following questions:

- What has changed at home and at school in this future?
- What has stayed the same at home and at school?
- What is important to the future you?
- What help might you need to keep reaching your goals in your future?

At times of transition, this activity can be particularly useful in helping plan provision that needs to be put in place.

When I'm older, I'd like to ...: Next, we want to know what the longer-term future might look like for the child. Katie was asked to draw a picture of herself when she is older. She created this in some detail using art materials, but this is not necessary. Katie then stuck post-it notes around her picture, saying what goals her future self would achieve. Her PCR champion encouraged her to think about what she might need in order to achieve the goals she had set, and who might be able to help her.

Activities for Question 6

Finally, we would like to know if the child has any questions they would like adults to think about or respond to at the PCR meeting. The following script can be used to encourage the child to think about what they might like to ask:

> At your meeting, there will be some people you know, such as your parents and teachers, and others you might not know. Everyone will be there to help you do your best at home and school. Can you think of anything you would like to ask these people during the meeting? Don't worry if you can't think of anything now, you will get another chance to add anything you've forgotten on the day.

The activities prepared for Katie and John both give them an idea of what they might expect at the PCR and allowed them time to think in advance about the questions that would be asked. It is common for children to think of new or different things they would like to say on the day, as both Katie and John did, and that is absolutely fine. Though Katie and John both used their completed activities with their respective PCR champions, Katie tended not to draw upon them much, whereas John copied his activities almost verbatim. In both cases, these activities gave them a valuable aide-memoire during the PCR.

Alternative tasks for early years and complex SEND

During our research we found that although the above tasks were suitable for the majority of children, they needed to be adjusted for others, such as those under 5 and those with complex, and particularly with communication-based, SEND. In addition, we worked with some, such as William, a young man in post-16 education with social interaction and communication needs, who were unable to access the elicitation activities discussed above. As his mother observes, other attempts must be made to ensure the inclusion of children and young people with such needs, so that they can feel fully part of the PCR process:

> **Parent:** I thought the meeting went very well, that the group that was there worked very well together, apart from William, who completely disengaged from the process, as I expected. I think if you are going to try and do this type of process with a young person on the [autism] spectrum, you have to meet that young person beforehand and understand a little bit about them, and

also then arrange to meet them in an environment they know and are comfortable with. Yes, he knows college, but he didn't know where he was in the college and he certainly didn't know the other people; even the college people in the room are not the people he normally deals with, so he was with a group of strangers basically.

In this case, elicitation packs and guidance on inviting professionals to the meeting were sent to the setting, but they had not been followed through. Clearly, it is important that the facilitator makes contact with the setting to ensure the pre-elicitation work has been completed, and to offer support with troubleshooting if necessary. One way of achieving this is through alternative means of gathering the child's views. This section is built on, or adapted from, work such as the Mosaic approach (Clark and Moss, 2011), puppet interview techniques (for example, Measelle *et al.*, 1998; Roth *et al.*, 2004) and total communication.

Using the PCR questions as a basis, the following activities are useful for gathering appropriate information.

- **Child tours:** Ask the child or young person to show you around their setting or home. Observe where they guide you to, their preferences, and their emotional and behavioural reactions to different areas, people, activities and so on. Note the words, phrases and other talk they use during the tour, and use these notes on their own or in triangulation with other activities.
- **Photographs/videos:** Give the young person a camera or video recorder and ask them to take photographs or video footage relevant to the PCR questions – for example, the activities, lessons or places they like or dislike. They could show their images to the people who support them, or to friends. If they produce non-sequential images or video footage, the adult will have to order it in preparation for the PCR meeting, or else provide a structure to what they photograph or video, such as interviews with people or collages or photograph books. Adults must utilize technology, such as cameras or iPads, sensitively, and ensure it is within their safeguarding protocols and practices.
- **Drama activities:** Activities such as role play, theatre games and methods such as Forum Theatre (Hammond, 2015a) can be helpful in eliciting the views of children and young people.

- **Parents and carers:** Talk with parents and carers – families will know the focus person best. Clear and open communication is essential to secure positive outcomes for the young people.
- **Puppets:** Puppet interviews can be a powerful way of communicating with children. The PCR champion should choose two identical puppets (or soft toys, if puppets are not available). Give them gender-neutral names such as 'Zok' and 'Zag' so as to minimize gender bias. Before the interview, draft a set of questions, such as 'Zok likes the playground; Zag does not like the playground. Which is most like you?' This will help to determine which areas of the school the child enjoys being in. Children can choose to point, touch, look or speak their answer. They may also wish to expand on it. These responses should be recorded.
- **Map-making:** Observation of younger children in early years settings can be extremely useful. Over at least two 30-minute time windows, the child's key worker starts by sketching out the layout of the setting; the key worker observes and plots the child's movements on the sketch, recording details such as the child's emotional and behavioural responses, the peers and adults the child seeks out for support and play, and the time the child spends on each activity.
- **Total communication:** This is a collection of approaches that is underpinned by a philosophy of empowering every person to communicate in the way they wish, to overcome any communicative barriers. The PCR champion has to be attuned and sensitive, and to know the focus person well. Approaches include: signs and symbols, talking mats, assistive technology, small-world play, picture exchange communication systems (PECS), presenting choices in accessible ways, art, music, writing, drawing, speech, and using concrete or photographed objects, non-verbal language including body language, gesture, movement and eye-gaze, and multi-sensory play such as model-making, painting and collages. A child who needs to use non-verbal ways of communicating should have a communication passport that can be shared as part of the PCR meeting.

  It is advisable not to ask the child how they wish to be communicated with. Doing so may appear to be person-centred, but asking such a question assumes the style within which the child wishes and is able to communicate. Instead, it is preferable to offer a range of approaches to the child from which they can choose.

The child's attendance at the PCR

It is generally desirable for the child to attend his or her entire PCR, but in certain circumstances this may do more harm than good. PCRs are *person-centred*, and no rule fits every child or situation. So discussions should be held with the child, where appropriate, and both parents or carers, about how much of the PCR the child should attend. For example, the child may have a life-limiting condition, social care circumstances or other needs of which they may be unaware, or which they would find distressing. Here, staff at Katie's school share their views based on several PCRs that were undertaken there:

> **Head:** I think it has been helpful when the child has been there for the affirmative part and has seen lots of positive comments made about them, so that gives them a real opportunity for that to happen. The two complex ones we had didn't have the child in the room anyway ...
>
> **CT:** No.
>
> **Head:** And I think for others that we have had, we have had the child in for part of the meeting, so generally I would say for part of the meeting would be the expected thing; obviously the last one, Katie, she stayed in for the whole meeting, and I didn't feel uncomfortable in that circumstance, because I think that was really quite helpful, so if we felt it wasn't helpful you would want to be able to really say, that's great you can go back to class now and not feel you could not say that, you know. I don't think it should just be down to the child making that decision.

Adults must make a judgement as to what is appropriate for the child, based on all the available information. For example, Katie and William stayed for their entire meetings, whereas John stayed through the affirmative part, returned to class and then came back to the PCR when the action plan had been completed. He was given the opportunity to agree to it or change aspects of it to ensure that the plan aligned with what he felt was relevant and achievable. While adults have to exercise a duty of care, this must be in line with the principles of person-centred practice.

It is generally important to encourage the child to attend their meeting, but they should be given a genuine choice about whether or not they do. They must on no account be penalized for not attending, nor be incentivized to attend. Where the resources included in this book are effectively used, most children are keen to come along. We also noticed that children who were subject to many, typically adult-driven, meetings, such as those used in social care, were reluctant about attending. However, given adequate preparation and support from key workers, they agreed to come along for a few minutes and then stayed for the entire meeting and, moreover, became actively involved.

Children and, where appropriate, parents or carers, have three broad options when considering how much of a PCR the child should attend:

1. None of the PCR. This option is discouraged wherever possible. Every effort should be made to have the child attend at least part of the meeting. Indeed, where developmentally appropriate, the child should have an equal say in contributing and agreeing to the action plan.
2. Part of the PCR. Typically, the child would be present at the start of the meeting. During the summary part of the process, the facilitator can take a natural pause after the question '*what is going well for the child?*', affording the adults a rest break, and facilitating the child's departure during adult conversations. But it is important that the child be invited back into the meeting towards the end, so that they can contribute and agree to the action plan. In practice, this is the most common approach.
3. All of the PCR. The child stays throughout the meeting. This is encouraged unless circumstances as described above apply. The adults must weigh up the benefits and risks to the child of attending the full PCR meeting.

Preparing adults

Adults also require preparation for a PCR. Once a PCR has been agreed, it is important to establish several details and preferences:

1. The name, date of birth, and year group of the child.
2. The contact person in the setting, and the PCR champion, if different.
3. Whether it is necessary to have a pre-consultation with the setting. This can be helpful if there is particularly sensitive information of which the facilitator should be aware, such as safeguarding concerns, whether the child is looked after by the local authority, and relevant details about the child's need.
4. Whether a visual or traditional report is required post-PCR. If you are a professional going into a setting, you will need to send a record of the PCR after the meeting. Typically, photographs are taken of the completed sheets of paper and prepared for distribution in a child-friendly report.

Alternatively, the setting may wish for a more traditional style of report. We discourage using a traditional report format, as explained later, alongside the child-friendly report template we offer.

5. Up to three key concerns the adults would like addressed during the PCR.

When a PCR is being held in an education setting, the SENDCo, setting manager or similar is expected to assume the role of coordinator of the PCR meeting. The following preparation checklist outlines the responsibilities of the coordinator and the activities that need to be delegated to someone else in the setting.

PREPARATION CHECKLIST

Before you elicit the child/young person's views, there are issues that you need to consider, and actions that may need to be taken before the meeting (see Box 2).

Box 2: Preparation checklists

Issue	Complete
We have identified who needs to be invited to the PCR and sent invitations.	
We have identified who cannot be invited (for example, due to known safeguarding issues).	
We have identified any potential complexities* and arrived at a solution (that is, consideration of LAC**, safeguarding and emotional needs).	
We have identified the limitations regarding what refreshments are available and the space/resource.	

*You should contact the PCR facilitator if you have any concerns, as adjustments to the PCR meeting or preparation activities might be required.

**We use the term LAC (looked-after children) broadly here, but as defined in the Children Act 1989. This means any child who has been in the care of the local authority for 24 hours or longer, such as children who have been fostered, are subject to a care order, or where the child attends a residential home or secure unit.

When you speak with the child and their parents or carers, please ensure that each of the points below is covered:

Issue	Complete
The child/young person and their family have received appropriate preparation (that is, accessed the online PCR film and visual guide).	
The child has been asked who they would like to be invited to the PCR (within adult boundaries set above).	
The child has been consulted on how they would like the room set up during the PCR, and the refreshments they would like (within adult boundaries set above).	
The child has been told about your role as PCR champion and that this will involve helping them before and during the PCR meeting.	
You have identified the child's preference for attendance (none, partial or full), in consultation with parents.	
The child is aware that what you discuss with them during the elicitation activities will be shared in the meeting.	

PROFESSIONALS' PCR AIDE-MEMOIRE

In addition to the preparation guide, we provided the professionals with a brief aide-memoire, distributed by email or in pigeon-holes, which was well received (see Box 3).

BOX 3: PROFESSIONALS' AIDE-MEMOIRE

A PCR will take place on __/__/__ at _____ for _____.

During the PCR, you will be asked to consider the following questions from **your** perspective:

1. What do you admire about the child?
2. What is going well for the child?
3. What is not working well for the child?
4. What is important to the child now?

5. What might be important to the child in the next 6–12 months?
6. Are there any questions you would like answered?

You are encouraged to answer these questions openly and honestly.

You might find it helpful to bring with you:

- Yourself! Please ensure you have cleared enough space in your diary to attend it all. PCRs usually take no longer than an hour but can last for up to two hours.
- Relevant reports on the child dated within the last 12 months.
- The child's current rate of progress *and* attainment.
- Your diary. We will be developing an action plan, which will require a review – a date for this review will be set at the meeting.

The PCR champion

> SENDCo: … because I was involved in the process of supporting John, I missed the opportunity to put down things for me in my role as SENDCo, whether that mattered or not, I don't know. Because actually what came out was what I would have put anyway, but it might do in other situations, I don't know.

The PCR champion is someone who knows the child well. However, as John's SENDCo reflects, this may be problematic, as the champion will also have a lot to contribute to the meeting. The PCR champion must therefore feel supported by the facilitator in their role, and must be given ample time to record their own views as well as supporting the child.

Preparing parents and carers

Parents and carers should typically receive a copy of the visual materials, access to the film, and resources such as a leaflet explaining the PCR process. How the parents receive this information is important. We posted information directly to parents, and followed this up with a phone call to make sure it had arrived and was understood. This was an effective approach. As Katie's mother reflects, the process was scary for parents, and perhaps would have been far scarier than it needed to be if this preparation had not been provided:

> Parent: I think that is what it was, it was the on the spot – oh my God, oh my God. You know, everyone was whipping round

[the questions] so quick, and I think I must have lapped it three times before I even answered one question.

Parents should be told who is coordinating the PCR – typically the SENDCo or similar – and have a contact number should they wish to contact them before the meeting.

Preparing the facilitator

The facilitator should also arrive prepared, and with seven large sheets of flip-chart paper with the following headings:

- PCR sign-in sheet
- What do we admire about X?
- What is going well for X?
- What is not working well for X?
- What is important to X now?
- What might be important to X in the next 6–12 months?
- Do you have any questions you would like answered?
- A 'live action plan'.

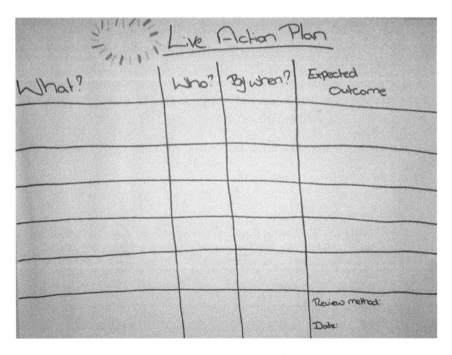

Figure 3.5: A pre-prepared live action plan. Photo by the authors.

Each sheet of paper has just the heading, except for the live action plan. Figure 3.5 shows a pre-prepared action plan without the child's name – add this in the coloured box preceding 'Live action plan' at the top of the sheet of paper.

The facilitator should also bring:

- Coloured pens (at least eight different colours)
- Blu Tack, to hang the sheets of paper
- Camera, to take photographs of the completed sheets after the PCR.

Arrival at a PCR

There was a standard approach to the start of PCRs for all the children with whom we worked. Once everyone was seated, the facilitator introduced himself, explained the process and read out a displayed set of ground rules, which are:

- There are no right or wrong answers. Don't worry about spelling or handwriting.
- Everyone's opinion is equal and valued. Everyone's views will be treated respectfully and without judgement.
- Free expression is encouraged. However, we ask that there is no shouting, swearing or aggressive behaviour.
- We will work together to look forward and think of realistic and relevant solutions.
- Everything shared today is confidential. If information is shared that may cause harm to you or others, this must be shared, but we will come to that if we need to.

At this stage, some key reminders were given, such as:

- The meeting will last for about an hour.
- At the end of the meeting the facilitator will take photos of the large sheets of paper and these will be shared in a child-friendly report. The report will be sent to those here today and anyone else we agree should see the report of this meeting.
- Confirm who in the room will be helping the child during the meeting – this is the PCR champion.
- Finally, ask those attending whether they have any questions before starting.

Chapter 4

Experiences of PCRs

> *Have you ever wondered?*
> *Well I have.*
> *About how when I say, say, red,*
> *For example there's no way of knowing if red*
> *Means the same thing in your head*
> *As red means in my head when someone says red*
>
> Tim Minchin, 'Quiet' (2010)

In this chapter, we follow Katie, John and their support networks as they experience the PCR process, and consider how the practicalities of the model can relate to other children with SEND and their families. We look at specific topics, starting with the role and actions of the facilitator, and continuing through to drawing up and reviewing an action plan. In addition to John, Katie and William, whose narratives appear in Chapter 3, we introduce Olivia, a primary-age child presenting with challenging attachment needs, and Ameera, a child in early years education, to explore these nuanced issues.

The facilitator
The skills of the facilitator

> **EP:** I think the process will work very successfully for certain groups or certain individuals, and if it is managed well and executed skilfully.

The facilitator needs to be skilful in running a PCR. They have to manage the process and the group dynamics, and drive the session towards an outcome-focused action plan. It is important that they act as a facilitator, not a leader or chairperson, who can work dynamically and flexibly, and with a clear focus on co-construction. They must assume a non-expert role, yet be able to use their expertise where relevant. The facilitator should demonstrate excellent consultation skills, and should be able to use the PCR process as a form of assessment. Educational psychologists are well placed to run such meetings, particularly within education settings, but other professional groups well positioned to work in this way include teachers, social workers and nurses. Most importantly, the professional must feel able to fulfil the complex role of facilitator, as the head and a class teacher (CT) involved in Katie's PCR discuss:

CT: It is a hugely skilled job, [but] ... your EP skills are not ones you are using necessarily, are they?

Head: But equally you are also reflecting on what's going on behind the statements.

CT: Absolutely.

Head: And I think [that for] someone without that psychology background, things might just be taken on a surface level as well.

CT: Yes, that is true.

As Katie's head teacher reflects, the facilitator must be sure not to fall into a procedural model (Smale *et al.*, 1993, 2000), and when identifying a facilitator, it is important to reflect on the impact this person will have on the meeting. For example, as John's SENDCo suggests, a PCR facilitated by a psychologist brings the professional application of psychology to a meeting:

SENDCo: ... the EP gives you a level of knowledge, expertise and understanding which you don't achieve via other meetings, [the] outcome is very positive ...

Some thought therefore needs to be given to the facilitator's professional background, but having the appropriate skill and flexibility to successfully facilitate the process is far more important.

From chairing to facilitation

SENDCo: I think the difference with the PCR is that there is a facilitator – there is no one voice that is stronger than any other voice – there is no one person necessarily as the lead role ...

The support networks in Katie's and John's cases all agreed that facilitation – as opposed to chairing – of the meeting was fundamental to its success. A facilitator is a neutral person who helps manage a group process, such as a PCR, in order to achieve a set objective (Thomas, 2010). There is a clear distinction between someone who facilitates and someone who chairs a meeting. Schwarz (2005) suggests that the task of the facilitator is to increase group effectiveness by improving the process (such as how the group works together), structure (such as ensuring that there are defined roles, responsibilities and guidance) and content (such as ensuring that the content of the PCR remains relevant to the objective of making an action plan). Facilitation promotes group autonomy and ownership, equalizes power distribution and promotes neutrality (Schwarz, 2005):

> **SENDCo:** [EP] was obviously able to facilitate, which adds another dimension, so it gives you an opportunity to stop, think, reflect at a deeper level than you would in just an annual review meeting or something like that. It provides structure but also open-endedness, where you can think and explore.

Katie's SENDCo suggests that the ability to facilitate, as opposed to chairing, a meeting has a profound impact on how PCRs are experienced. Many of the processes to support children and families claim to be person-centred, such as annual review meetings for children with SEND, personal education plan (PEP) meetings for children who are looked after by a local authority, and Signs of Safety meetings, which aim to build on strengths within families to safeguard children. All these processes have a place in supporting children and families, and include the child's views to a greater or lesser extent, but all are chaired, not facilitated. This means that the person within the process becomes part of an adult-driven procedural event that moves away from being truly person-centred. This sentiment is highlighted by Katie's SENDCo, who was involved in several PCRs that we ran:

> **SENDCo:** … I think parents have definitely appreciated that it is being led by an EP, because they have said it is a very different experience to what they have had before, and all of them have been through the FSP process.

It is vital that the facilitator remains neutral in the process. In a bid to be efficient when providing access to PCRs, it is common for SENDCos and head teachers to consider running PCRs in-house themselves. This causes problems in terms of both role definition and participation. As Katie's head teacher observes, the external facilitator is able to provide a space for everyone to reflect by reframing comments and repositioning situations in order to move forward:

> **Head:** … the person who is leading the PCR needs to be highly skilled [otherwise] I think it could go wrong. [The facilitator is] effectively listening to the comments and reflecting at the time that people are writing and bringing things together, so I do think it is very much dependent on who, you know, I think there are all sorts of cases like this, you know, how it is led …

As the PCR is effectively a dynamic form of consultation, the facilitator must be distanced from the context. During the process, the facilitator draws together multiple stories without applying their own agenda to the conclusions drawn. Gently clarifying points made, and encouraging the group to reflect and make sense of the information being presented while helping to guide the process, can significantly contribute to positive experiences for the group (Schwarz, 2005).

However, the challenge for the facilitator goes beyond remaining neutral and managing the process. Occasionally, conflict, tension and hostility arise within a PCR because relationships break down, safeguarding is an issue, or there is conflict over how the situation is perceived. The ground rules should help to contain such situations, and the facilitator must work sensitively to ensure that everyone's views are captured and worked through, as one of John's class teachers remarks:

> CT: ... I guess the danger is that stuff that should be said doesn't get said, and if everybody feels like that ... you don't want that to happen. I suppose we all have to be just a bit brave about it, and maybe it needs saying at the beginning ... everybody was really respectful. It's just hard, hard things need to be said, and that's just hard, probably, and not an easy way around it.

It is important that everyone has the support to share how they feel. If they do not, people may feel a lack of ownership or be dissatisfied with the action, and so become less committed to implementing it. Hence, the facilitator needs to promote a sense of trust, openness and honesty among the participants – for which neutrality is key.

The importance of a personable facilitator

It is true to say that PCRs will not suit everyone's approach to practice, and that not everyone will find facilitation easy. Not only training, but also professional identity, personal beliefs, values and general approach to meeting need will determine the suitability of the facilitator to run a PCR. The PCR facilitator may well bring their expertise to the process, but must step away from assuming a role of expert. Equally, one must critically reflect on how person-centred one's practice is, and how this fits with what the PCR process demands. Above all, what matters is the atmosphere created by the facilitator, and the way in which sensitive issues are managed. Inevitably, the experiences of the PCR are enhanced when the facilitator is personable:

SENDCo: It is really important that it is done in that non-judgemental climate where the focus is on what we can all do for the child, rather than proving a theory about poor parenting.

Parent: Yes, if he [the facilitator] had been more official – do you know what I mean? If he had been that sort of, not uptight, but that official figure looking – it wouldn't have worked. It wouldn't, because Katie wouldn't have spoken to him like she did, and I don't think I would have been comfortable speaking to him the way I did either. So yes, definitely. Go [name of facilitator]!

During the course of her PCR, Katie shared with the group that her mother was 'moody'. The facilitator noticed how uncomfortable this made Katie's mother, and handled it lightly so as to minimize embarrassment and normalize the concept of being 'moody'. Katie's mother says that this went a long way to making her experience of the PCR positive:

Parent: … [name of facilitator] just laughed it off as well, didn't he? But if he hadn't, I probably would have cried, to be honest, and I would have felt uncomfortable then, and I probably would have made other people feel uncomfortable, and I probably would have then left and not come back. Because it was horrible.

SENDCo: … yes, it doesn't feel very nice.

Parent: It didn't, no. I didn't like that part, I must say, I didn't like that.

We should not forget that often it is the little things that make all the difference. Facilitators should also remember that those invited to the PCR are often new to the PCR situation. Typically, the PCR process is still an unusual way of working in a school and, although this has its benefits, it can make people feel vulnerable. The facilitator must therefore provide containment, and manage often conflicting and strong emotional responses from those attending.

The facilitator's role in managing emotional responses

Containment is thought to occur when one person receives and understands the emotional communication of another without being overwhelmed by it, processes it and then communicates understanding and recognition back to the other person. This process can restore the capacity to think in the other person. (Douglas, 2007: 33)

PCRs can be a highly emotional experience. Many parents whose children have had a PCR reported feeling heard and empowered by the process – some after many years of feeling they had to fight to get support. Emotions can run high; it is the facilitator's role to contain such emotions and ensure the process remains constructive and forward-thinking. This is not easy, as one of Katie's teachers says:

> CT: ... I can see situations where as [the head teacher] was saying it, it has the potential to get confrontational if there isn't somebody very strong there to hold it all together. There are some quite challenging and difficult things that people quite rightly want to say, and it is quite right to get those out in the open. [But] I think it is quite dependent on the person who is running it to be strong enough to be able to deal with those kinds of complex relationships, because there are lots of complicated relationships in the room.

Thomas (2008) argues that because of such complexities, facilitators need to have a strong sense of self-awareness in order to deal with group dynamics. They are often responding to emotional reactions that echo their own response to what is being discussed (Schwarz, 2005). The facilitator must understand that their own emotional responses, and how these impact on group behaviour, are just as important. Creating a safe space for the PCR relies on the interconnected skills of being self-aware, reflexive, reflective and able to offer containment. However, one does not have to be a psychologist to have these skills, nor will psychologists necessarily make good facilitators, even though educational psychologists, particularly, are often well positioned to run PCRs. What is most important is that the facilitator is both skilled in managing the process and able to be sensitive to the emotions of others. As John's SENDCo explains:

> SENDCo: ... it relies on an extremely skilled EP to manage it, and he was very skilled in the way he drew the information out from you without actually making it feel personal, because it genuinely wasn't. But in the hands of another, less skilled, EP, that could have gone very pear-shaped, and also potentially in the hands of a SENDCo that hadn't really made the connection and had made a set of judgements about that parent and was using the meeting as an excuse to prove their set of judgements about that parent, it could go pear-shaped. That's my feeling.

When facilitated well, PCRs offer greater flexibility than traditional approaches, so they feel quite different from other school experiences. John's mother observed that:

> **Parent:** ... it's a relaxed process; you are not under pressure to do anything ... I don't know how to explain, it was more, like when you go into a clinic it is very structured – this was more wibbly-wobbly if you like. You could put in any bit and say what you wanted, and you felt like someone was actually listening. Whereas before, anything I have gone to, I would say something and someone would come back at me with 'oh, this is the way we do it' kind of thing. I didn't feel like there was anybody listening, if you like, but with this [PCR] system I feel like my voice is being heard.

An effective PCR helps redistribute power, allowing parents, who so often feel disempowered by SEND systems, to regain their voice. In order to move stuck situations forward, the facilitator must read the room well enough to offer containment but also be assertive, and draw together complex and competing narratives and identify the people who will drive the action plan forward beyond the PCR. Katie's mother noticed this:

> **Parent:** I was glad that other people could see what I could see. I liked the fact that, as much as me and [SENDCo] had tried to get things moving, we needed somebody else to come in and give that extra kick up the bum. [The facilitator] did that by him giving people in that room [actions] – 'can you do this', 'can you do that' – he was setting people tasks, and without that we wouldn't have then moved on, you know, we wouldn't have moved further ahead so we needed him to come in and just give us that extra push. Now some of the people who weren't listening to what Katie's needs were will now listen ... [It] will make a huge amount of difference to Katie. Him just coming in has made a huge amount of difference, to be honest; the report itself, I think, will be the final touch, but just him being here has made all the difference, definitely.

Experiencing the PCR process
Equalizing power distribution
There is generally an implicit power imbalance between the professional and the parents, so that one or the other withholds privileged information

to satisfy their own agendas. It is not unusual for a professional or parent to approach the chairperson immediately after a meeting has ended to offer information that they felt unable to share in the meeting, or for the professionals involved to meet without the child's parents knowing. Although it is occasionally appropriate for professionals to meet to discuss a child when, for example, there are serious safeguarding concerns, such meetings should not be a way to reinforce the professionals' power. But traditional professional-led meetings do form part of the norm in schools, and so PCRs and collaborative meetings may initially feel uncomfortable. John's teacher and SENDCo said:

> **CT:** I was a bit nervous to start with because I wasn't quite sure how the parents were going to react to professionals speaking, and I know parents are there at some of the meetings normally, but perhaps not necessarily all of them. I was just a bit nervous of, perhaps, the type of language I might use, or the exact things I might say or whatever, and I was saying to you I didn't know whether to write this or not ... I think it is just getting over it, that's the important thing. Not to mean that I would lie to the parents, I don't mean that at all, but, you know, I would word it slightly differently ...

> **SENDCo:** ... there were some things that I was saying to [the facilitator] that I knew and I was thinking, is it relevant to put it on [the large sheet of paper], which I felt it was, but I wasn't sure how it would be received by the parents.

PCRs are a transparent process. Attendees are asked specific questions and are encouraged to respond openly and honestly on the large sheets of paper provided. This transparency is a strength as it allows for open dialogue, and this can facilitate moving previously stuck situations forward. However, it also relies on trust and openness from all involved, and it requires professionals to be comfortable about relinquishing any implicit power they hold. Some participants might feel uneasy about sharing information. Equally, the simultaneous methods of recording one's thoughts may inhibit participants who would normally conform to an emerging group consensus, particularly where organizational hierarchies are well established, such as in schools. Noelle-Neumann (1974) proposed a theory of the spiral of silence, where people adjust their own behaviour and opinions to conform to those of the group, or do not voice their opinion at all, in case they become isolated (Scheufele, 2008; Shoemaker *et al.*, 2000). Studies of social conformity also give clues to how uncomfortable a PCR process might be – it is not possible to conform to an idea if those ideas are recorded independently and simultaneously for all to see. PCRs shift the psychological experience of traditional meetings to very different discussions and outcomes. Not having a group consensus to comply with may be liberating for those involved, and could go some way to equalizing the distribution of power. As this EP attending John's PCR comments:

> **EP:** … if someone else is saying something out loud in a meeting, it is kind of out there and we know about that kind of group thing, and stuff like that. Skilled people in traditional meetings know when to say something and what to say and, so, in a sense, [PCRs] provide a bit of an easier space where people might feel happier to write something down to something else that is quite contradictory, than to say it in a meeting … if you are just free to write your own bullet points you don't even have to read what somebody else has written if you don't want to, whereas you do have to hear what somebody else has to say in a meeting because that is the way it runs.

The facilitator must nevertheless work sensitively to support and encourage participants to be open and honest, and must be so themselves. The ground rules should be followed, and the bullet points recorded on the sheets of paper should be read aloud by the facilitator, so that everyone's views are heard by the time an action plan is pulled together. During the preparation stages, the adults should mention any issues that concern them, so that the facilitator can support them when these are shared during the PCR. Equalizing power is not the same as creating a power imbalance in favour of those assumed to be oppressed. The object is to create conditions that allow everyone to participate as fully as possible:

> **SENDCo:** … it kind of felt safe, and perhaps she [parent] saw it very much as a supportive mechanism, whereas meetings we have had with that particular parent before … it was defensive, it was fighting for something. This was sort of a meeting where everyone is there with John; we sat there talking about him, putting him in the middle and saying how do we best respond, so she obviously felt very safe to kind of expose and say I need some help here.

The facilitator needs to move skilfully between providing what the group needs at any time while remaining person-centred and outcome-focused. White (2005) advocates the therapeutic posture, where the therapist, or the facilitator, responds mindfully to what emerges in the space in order to challenge, empower, support ownership and, where necessary, act within policy, procedure and laws to protect and refer on:

> **Head:** ... there is a real openness, the openness is really good and, occasionally, it is challenging too. It touches on safeguarding issues, and then there is a bit of awkwardness around that as well, particularly if a child is in the room, for example, or a child has said something and it is plastered up there ...

Katie's head teacher, who had been involved with several PCRs, rightfully raises the issue of safeguarding, during the preparation activities with the child or during the PCR itself. In such cases, the facilitator has to take a more authoritative position and adopt a procedural model (for example, Sanderson and Lewis, 2012; White, 2005; Smale *et al.*, 1993, 2000). It is important to achieve a balance between empowering and encouraging a child's sense of agency, while also fulfilling our duty of care to support and protect them (Devecchi *et al.*, 2015).

The role of co-construction in PCRs

Individual knowledge and cultural understanding, norms, values and beliefs are integrated to form a collective knowledge (Mayordomo and Onrubia, 2015). The co-construction of knowledge is a social phenomenon (Burr, 2015). PCRs provide a space for co-construction to take place through various strategies, such as the participants using distinctively coloured pens to write their views on the sheets of paper:

> **EP:** I did like the different coloured pens ... it was a nice touch, it was nice and clear around the room which bit you had written on ... I thought it made it a bit more interesting for the child, as I think she quite liked looking at what everybody had written about her, and the teacher was reading the comments back about what other people had put and guiding her to these comments on paper – that was really good.

Unlike in more traditional meetings, the views of the participants are presented as they intend them, and are subject only to self-editing, and are not reinterpreted or edited before being recorded. During the summary part of the PCR process, the facilitator can clarify personal constructs of vague terms, such as 'friends', diagnostic labels – so we can identify need beyond the label – and within-child concepts, such as 'resilient', 'kind', 'naughty' or 'rude'. This allows for socially constructed meanings to be better understood, so that all participants can move forward with confidence and clarity.

The psychological–philosophical model of embodied cognition has a place in PCRs, concerned as it is with cognitive skills such as thinking, reasoning and information processing, and how they are stimulated through acting within our world (Shapiro, 2011; Clark, 1997). PCRs are active and interactive. Sitting is discouraged; the participants are on their feet, writing down on paper their answers to the questions on the board and interacting with one another. Such interacting stimulates these cognitive processes, and thinking becomes visible. A specialist learning support teacher (SLST) who attended John's PCR observes:

> **SLST:** ... I thought that the questions that were put around the room on paper, which people then wrote their answers on, were very useful, and making thinking visible was very helpful. I suppose being able to look again at what had been put in the different areas was helpful, so that one could think again and add to what one had said, and think about what other people had said and reflect on that, and that was good. It just felt very efficient and constructive, and that one was working towards something that would be a very workable way forward for the child, and a shared understanding of where the strengths and difficulties were, and what could help to move things on.

John's parent agrees with the SLST. She reflects on how the participants' dynamic response to key questions allowed her to think differently about the situation:

> **Parent:** ... it was good because you see what other people thought, and a lot of them were things that I was thinking about as well, so I knew that people were on the same wavelength as me. We were all, like, writing down our thoughts and ideas about it, and when you went around you could see that everybody was on the same wavelength by what they were writing down. Which was good; it was the first time that I felt that people were on the same wavelength because when you go to all these different things, you have got a bit of this and a bit of that, and nothing seems to gel. But here, everybody is writing down their thoughts and their ideas, and they were all sort of merging together, so I then knew that everybody was all thinking the same thing, which was good, and best for me I think.

Undertones to John's mother's reflections suggest that the focus on the child, the transparency of the process and the simultaneous recording of responses all contributed to the sense of a joint purpose and equal power. The dynamic nature of a PCR can be extremely powerful:

> **EP:** [one of the] strengths is that there is a different way of doing things. So, if participants have had poor experiences in the past of meetings, then I think it provides a fresh opportunity to let us revisit this idea, the concept of a meeting, so that's good. I think not everybody likes sitting still and some people really like to move around, and I think it's that whole thing about kinaesthetic, that, you know, movement can free up thought and emotion, and it's a bit like the reasons why we do the kinaesthetic family drawings, for example. Or why we do yoga, you know, on a personal level, or other exercise – it is because it takes our thinking and feeling to a slightly different plane, if you like. So, I think that is very good.

We thought about how children might respond in PCR meetings should they wish to contribute something not recorded on the pre-elicitation activities. We were keen that the child's participation went beyond tokenism (Hart, 1992). The literature suggests that drawing can be helpful (for example, Sanderson and Lewis, 2012), so we made it our starting point for supporting children to engage with, and learn about, meaning-making and co-construction, skills that are vital to education (Bruner, 1996).

Children's drawings support their communication, and the technique is well regarded (for example, Farokhi and Hashemi, 2011). Drawings have been used to explore children's perceptions of attention deficit hyperactivity disorder (ADHD) diagnosis (Kenny, 2016), to assess lived experiences (Di Leo, 2013) and engagement in theatre performances (Reason, 2010), and extensively by psychologists in work with children (Ravenette, 1999). Children's drawings are the basis on which co-construction of their views can take place. When the child is unable or unwilling to expand on their drawing, other sources of information, such as the pre-elicitation activities and knowledge of the child from those attending the PCR, can be drawn together to create meaning, and the key points can be recorded by the facilitator to form a follow-up report. Ravenette (1999) argues that a drawing will have multiple meanings, depending on who is viewing it, but they can still provide information about the child's views when co-constructing knowledge within the PCR. The psychologist attending Katie's meeting observes that arts-based approaches are meaningful in PCRs:

EP: ... I think for people who do feel comfortable and able to make marks that aren't words or phrases, I think it is lovely to give them that opportunity. I wonder how you would convert those kinds of recordings meaningfully, and giving them equal value to, say, words or statements, or bullet points, in the traditional way.

Katie chose to record her thoughts in drawings as well as key words. The facilitator paid careful attention to these drawings, and used them in discussions with Katie and those who knew her well. The result was a narrative about how Katie felt about each question posed. For example, she drew a playground scene under the question 'What is working well?' In discussions it was agreed that the playground was a good place for Katie to be: she had friends, and enjoyed playing on a particular apparatus; she knew who to go to if things went wrong, but we also gathered that Katie had a limited sense of danger. However, caution is needed when interpreting drawings: be sensitive to cultural differences, and ensure that every artwork receives the same weight as the words gathered in the PCR, and that this balance is maintained in subsequent reports.

The expertise of all the participants, including children, needs to be included in planning ways forward (for example, Realpe and Wallace, 2010; Parks *et al.*, 1981); in England and Wales, this is a legal responsibility under the Children and Families Act 2014 and the associated SEND guidance (DfE/DoH, 2015: 46). The deputy head teacher of Katie's school reflects:

DH: ... it wasn't an isolated thought process, I wasn't in a room filling in boxes, I was with everybody else and we were all doing it together. I think because when you are filling in boxes there is all the bits that you could miss ... you don't get a feel, necessarily, for the person that you are talking about. But when that child is in the room, and just by the things that Katie was doing, and even [children who have had a PCR from] reception age, you can begin to get a feel about that person. Everybody could begin to get a feel for what Katie [and other children] was like.

Action plans that are co-produced are more likely to result in sustainable change (Cahn, 2004), although as we have seen they can be limited by the cultures within which change is being attempted (see, for example, Stephens *et al.*, 2008). PCRs provide a space where co-construction is enabled by a transparent, accountable and well-managed process, as staff in Katie's school note:

> **SENDCo:** ... I think one of the really good things about it, is you have got everyone in the room together; everyone knows what everyone else is saying. It's not, kind of, one group of people saying one thing that they wouldn't say in front of the parents, you know.

> **DH:** ... it just felt as though everybody was working towards the same goal, there was nobody that knew any better than anybody else; it just to me personally made it feel as though everybody was at the same level, the same place, and heading in the same direction, without a kind of distinction between 'this is a SENDCo', 'this is a class teacher', and 'this is a parent' – it just felt that we were all the one voice for that child.

Smale and colleagues (1993, 2000) refer to such sharing of expertise as an exchange model. This is in contrast to expert-driven meetings, such as the more traditional questioning and procedural models. The exchange model can be a powerful experience, as discussed by staff from Katie's setting:

> **Head:** I think it gave us a chance to see and all talk about the child from all different aspects, and I think we got a better knowledge of the child back at home and at school. I think that was a good platform for that, so I think that is a strength ...

> **CT:** I would agree.

> **Head:** But I understood the parents more. I understood how the child related to the parents and each particular issue they were dealing with as well. So, I think that is actually really very helpful and at the same time didn't break down the relationship between the parent and the school, and, you know, that is helpful.

John's mother was also pleased with the benefits of the exchange model and the impact it had on her child, and particularly on his ability to reflect on what goals to pursue and to draw upon his own expertise when thinking about the action plan:

> **Parent:** ... I think the inclusion of John in it was really good, because it helped him to understand himself a bit better as well, when he was going around writing things down. So I think it is very good for the children, the way it is done, it is extremely good for the children because it makes them think about what they want and what they want to achieve, and to understand why they

can't. They are included in it, they are not just saying we have decided we are going to do this – he was there and he could have his input as well, so I think that was really good.

The value of including the child's views, and the sense of ownership that involvement offers the child, especially in the action plan, should not be underestimated.

PCRs as a family-centred practice

Parent: I was hoping that there would be somebody there to listen, and that there would be something put in place, as I went in with small expectations. But I came out with so much more; there is this system that is so good for the whole family.

Being centred on a focus person, the PCR must be used in a way that situates that person within the systems in which they operate. Kurt Lewin, a psychologist interested in the interaction between the person, their environment and their subsequent behaviour, said:

Every scientific psychology must take into account whole situations, i.e., the state of both person and environment. This implies that it is necessary to find methods of representing person and environment in common terms as part of one system. (Lewin, 1936: 12)

Therefore, it is not possible to be *person-centred* in isolation from the wider context. The head teacher in John's school reflects on how the PCR can provide a holistic view of the family and the challenges presented at home, and of how to support the child's education:

Head: ... it very much can reflect the initial early help discussions and actually going in with a child and a child psychology element; we got as much out in terms of what we could do going forward to support families. We probably got more out of it because it wasn't about 'you being bad as a parent' or 'you being poor or neglectful' or 'your debit crisis is seriously impacting on your child's capacity to cope in school', so in that respect it was more productive in terms of child protection for me, in terms of child protection.

Many of those who attend a PCR find that the process offers the flexibility, informality and sense of safety that allow them to speak freely about the difficulties that occur outside the school. PCRs become family-centred by equalizing power and promoting collective ownership between home, school and the child:

> **Head:** … I felt it is a different and fresher approach to gaining information, and about children and their families. I like the way the children and the adults and the parents of those are equally as involved in the process at the same time, or they have listed their views prior to the occasion. I do like the way everyone is listened to, so I do think the protocols do enable everybody to have an equal share of what is going on.

> **EP:** … it felt like everybody had a way to include their views, and I really liked how the child's views felt equal to everybody else's. I think sometimes in meetings children's views are just kind of gathered as a kind of checklist, but actually the child being there and being able to write things on the wall, and that being facilitated quite nicely, I liked how that was included. It was very good. I was very impressed.

Those who were involved in John's and Katie's PCRs, and had experienced other PCRs run by the facilitators, were impressed with the way in which all the children's views were successfully included; they felt that other processes in which they had been involved compared very unfavourably. Including the child in the ways allowed by PCRs builds up a family-orientated approach in which parents and adults see the child as a competent, autonomous agent:

> **Parent:** … I liked that she, she loved it as well. I was in a meeting and she liked it that she felt involved, that she got to write her own bit. A lot of it wasn't really that focused on the question, just a bit out there, but that is Katie.

Katie's mother found it very useful that Katie was equally involved in the PCR. However, there is a risk that the child might not answer the questions set. Preparation activities are vital to ensure that they do. It is also vital to assign a suitable PCR champion, and for the facilitator to ensure that equal consideration is given to all commentary from the child, however irrelevant it might seem. In this way, the voice of the child contributes significantly to unsticking situations at home, possibly even those deemed too difficult for the adults to address, or those that fall outside adult-driven constructs:

> **Head:** I thought the process was really strong. I think the child's voice is vital; in fact, the child's voice was extremely strong, you know, where it generated ideas about her own dealing of

anxieties around bereavement and those sorts of ideas. Katie was talking about things nobody else had overly considered, because we get thrown by, you know, is this child dyslexic, you know, or is this child coping with a [possible] ASD diagnosis. So, where a child's voice is a very strong component, it challenges all of us, you know, that is really vital. I think where a child is allowed to speak, that a child's voice is allowed to be equal, that's really important – if people actually look at what the child is actually saying, you know, if two participants had looked at what the child was actually saying, it could have altered the quality of the action plan.

Because the PCR process has to be balanced to ensure the needs of the child are met, it moves between being child-centred and family-centred. John's father explains:

> Parent: … if you are just child-centred, then you, especially with the younger children and especially with children [who] have any sort of learning disability, whether it is an ASD, or, you know, a developmental delay or some other respect, they may not have a very good idea of what happens to them aside from their own sort of feelings about it, or even their abilities to express those feelings. So, I think it might be better to say family-centred.

The facilitator must avoid playing into vulnerability discourses. The task is to ensure that the child is given sufficient agency to express their views, and have them incorporated into the action plan, while also making appropriate suggestions or recording decisions that are adult-driven. The occupational therapist (OT) who attended John's PCR suggests that the process can remain child-centred without being child-led:

> OT: … it was a clear explanation of what we were supposed to be doing, and the facilitator importantly made John feel really involved as well, which I think was really important. It was a useful activity to do in terms of thinking of the child as a whole, and seeing what his needs are and what his strengths and difficulties are, and also it helped the child think quite positively about himself, which was really nice.

Including the child can occasionally be very challenging, especially if the child has been poorly prepared and has a specific need, such as complex social interaction and communication difficulties. Below, a mother whose son, William, underwent a PCR speaks about him. At age 17, he was attending a post-16 setting. William's preparation for the PCR, carried out by the PCR champion, was insufficient, which, given the nature of his needs, caused him some stress:

> **Parent:** … he is writing here about memory, what will be important for William in the foreseeable future. I mean, he actually doesn't realize that he doesn't actually know about how to do these questions and we have got a young man now, who's just 17 coming up to 18, who really has no sense of who he is or where he is going in life or what he is doing. He is scared rigid about his future and where he is going. And so, talking about what is important to him, improving long-term, short-term memory, that has been important his whole life, and yet he is not able to, he is not at a point where he can. Lots of young people, they don't know the answers, but he's really not able to sort of cope with that title, you are not actually getting, if all the professionals that are in the room with him, I don't think you are getting a lot out of him, do you know what I mean?

In circumstances such as William's, encouraging the child to have agency is likely to be the ideal rather than the reality. Preparation, and the PCR itself, should, as far as possible, encourage an appropriate degree of autonomy. Placing the process within a wider, family-based, context can extend ownership and promote success of implementation. This is critical, considering when the child will return to a far less child-centred context. We need parents, and the other adults who attend the PCR, to be signed up to the action plan, and to ensure that the child remains protected and that all the actions are taken in the child's best interests (see, for example, Sanderson and Lewis, 2012). Moreover, a family-centred process is likely to alleviate the stress on the child and accommodate any SEND that might prevent engagement.

Take, for example, children who have social interaction and communication difficulties, such as autism. Some of these children find difficulty imagining or future-thinking. For example, a question to William about what might be important to him in 12 months' time was difficult for him to engage with. Younger children such as Katie also found this concept a little tricky. Some children with SEND struggle to recognize their own difficulties, and therefore may struggle to answer other problem-focused questions accurately.

The challenges around transition faced by William are not uncommon, and usually cause confusion and anxiety, so planning for their future is essential (Stoner *et al.*, 2007). It is necessary and possible to involve young people with social interaction and communication difficulties in planning their futures, but this needs to be carefully handled by settings and the services that work with them (Hodgetts and Park, 2017). The ways in which we engage young people such as William, however, are likely to be slightly different to the ways we have discussed in relation to Katie and John. Visual-based preparation activities, described in Chapter 3, may be helpful to young people like William, but others can be used within the PCR to help children who have SEND. Figures 4.1 and 4.2 are visuals that we have used in PCRs to help children, including those with social interaction and communication needs, to access questions.

Figure 4.1: 'What is working well' wall display visual

Figure 4.2: 'What do we admire about' wall display visual

Involving parents and carers in the education and future planning for their child should be a priority. This not only supports the child in sharing views when the presenting SEND makes this tricky, but also helps generally to develop plans and improve outcomes. Involving the parent in contributing to the construction of knowledge that surrounds the problem and solution in any situation affords a sense of ownership and understanding that can lead to a greater sense of collaboration and mutual support between home and setting:

> **DH:** ... I think for the parents as well, they were kind of so involved with the process, I was speaking to somebody yesterday who was saying that when a parent is involved with a medical profession, they are involved in so much of what goes on but in education the door somehow slightly shuts. So, the parent doesn't really know sometimes what is going on, because they are not in the classroom with the child. So, actually, to be with a group of people that know their child really well and being able to move

around and just actually have those little incidental conversations as you are doing it, just a clarity of thought and certainly for the professionals, you are talking things through aloud and just trying to clarify your thinking, so it is a good support network ...

This kind of family-centred ethos complements a person-centred process. The depth of co-construction, support and understanding that can be fostered through empowering these kinds of contributions should not be underestimated. The psychologist who observed John's PCR reflects:

> EP: ... the parent felt she was listened to and she felt that John was listened to, and I don't think she had had that beforehand, in such a collaborative way. The teacher came back and said that mum had felt that it was the most positive meeting she had had, because she was able to, and, I felt, ... they were allowed to share as much as they felt comfortable with, which I thought was a really nice way of making sure that everyone felt confident enough to share what they wanted. I think that worked particularly well with that mum, and for John as well; she felt quite positive that he was able to share what he wanted.

Documentation in PCRs: Action plans and outcomes
Action plan and reporting

Along with the sheets of paper on the walls, the PCR results in an action plan, which is photographed and put into a child-friendly report. The action plan is created and owned by those who attend the PCR, so the information and actions are clearly communicated. The SENDCo in Katie's case remarks on the benefits of this approach:

> SENDCo: Everybody is in the same place at the same time, and has had the same message and has the same action plan. There's not the potential confusion over who said they would do what, and there isn't any arguing with it: you were all there and you all heard what was said, and this is what we are going to do about it. I think that is a massive strength.

A PCR action plan lists the following key information:

- *What the action will be*: this must be clear and measurable, and include at least some indication of the provision that is needed to fulfil the action.
- *Who* takes responsibility for ensuring the action is completed.

- *By when* can we reasonably expect the action to be completed.
- What is our *expected outcome* and how we will know if the action has been successful. This should include clear and measurable success criteria. The Code of Practice states that the outcome must show the *benefit or difference made to an individual as a result of an intervention* (DfE/DoH, 2015: 46).

Settings vary in the way they record and monitor progress for children in their care. The action plan provides enough information for settings to incorporate it into existing templates or systems, such as IEPs or provision maps. Below is an example of an action plan target, as drawn up in Katie's action plan:

> **Context:** the attendees would like Katie to be able to read consonant–vowel–consonant (c–v–c) words before the next review in six weeks' time.
>
>> **What:** for Katie to access precision teaching ten minutes, daily, to practise high-frequency c–v–c words.
>>
>> **Who:** initials of the person who will be responsible for the intervention, plus the class teacher and SENDCo who will have an overview of the intervention.
>>
>> **By when:** start immediately, with review in six to eight weeks' time.
>>
>> **Expected outcome:** to read at least ten c–v–c words fluently and accurately in at least two contexts – classroom and intervention.

When well facilitated, child-centred and collaborative, action plans become a gold standard in personalizing education for children with SEND.

Post-PCR, the action plan is distributed to attendees along with other information collected during the meeting on the child-friendly report. Box 4 shows a template for this report.

Box 4: Child-friendly PCR report

<u>My PCR</u>

CHILD'S NAME:
(DOB: --.--.----)

<u>Background</u>
- My Person-Centred Review (PCR) took place at [SETTING] on [DATE].
- A member of staff from the setting's pastoral team met me a couple of days before to gather my views. These were fed into my PCR meeting.
- I attended all of my PCR/I attended part of my PCR/I did not attend my PCR (delete as applicable).
- My PCR was facilitated by [facilitator's name], a [facilitator's job title/position] for [name of the organization the facilitator belongs to].

<u>Understanding my PCR report</u>

This is a **very special report** because it has been written with me as **part of a team** and is made up of **my views,** and those of [names of others who attended]. The first part of the report uses photos of all the writing and drawings everyone did on the large sheets of paper hung around the room. These photos are important because they show that everyone in the team has an *equal and valued voice* in the PCR process – including me.

[*In the UK, psychologists are required by the Health Care Professions Council (HCPC) to provide a written formulation of their involvement, and hypotheses about what might be happening in the presenting circumstances. The following paragraph can be added to indicate that an additional summary is included at the end of the report to fulfil this criterion.*]

At the end of this report [name of the facilitator] has written a special summary for adults to read. This summary pulls together key themes from the meeting and uses psychology to present ideas about what might be happening in my situation and provide additional ways we might move forward together.

<u>Here are the people who attended my PCR</u>

*** Add photo of PCR register here ***

Everyone wrote in a different colour, so we knew who made which comments on the large sheets of paper. My colour was [write the colour of child's pen here in the same colour as the pen].

We then went around the room and filled in our answers to questions on the large sheets of paper. My views were based on some of the activities I'd completed before the meeting, but also some new things I wanted to share on the day. Here is what everyone said:

***Add photo of **'what we admire about ...'** ***
***Add photo of **'what is going well for...'** ***
***Add photo of **'what is not working well for ...'** ***
***Add photo of **'what is important to ... now'** ***
***Add photo of **'what might be important to ... in the next 6–12 months'** ***
***Add photo of **'questions we'd like answered'** ***
***Add photo of **'live action plan'** ***

And this is my action plan! It was agreed that there would be a review on [add date]. This review will take place between ... and .... [name those who have agreed to attend], but other people might be invited too, if they need to be there. My review will take place at [add location] and will be run as a [add either PCR, if you intend to review the PCR with another PCR, or the method of in-house review process, such as an IEP review].

[*As per the formulation paragraph above, if the PCR has been facilitated by a psychologist or another professional obliged to write a formulation or summary of their work and hypotheses, the following section is included; otherwise, it can be omitted.*]

<u>Psychological formulation</u>

Thank you for asking me to facilitate [name of child]'s PCR; it was my pleasure to meet you and [name of child] during my visit.

Summarize key points
Provide professional formulation and hypotheses
Add additional suggestions or indicate that the action plan is sufficient

Signed: **Dated:**

The report template makes it straightforward for you to populate the sections that are highlighted with either information that arose from the process or the photographs taken. Writing from a first-person perspective and providing photographs in place of a traditional report can take some getting used to. Adults can find it difficult to look at documents through the eyes of a child, and may feel that the report might be less authoritative than traditional forms of reporting. In Katie's case:

> **Head:** ... somebody challenged [the report], I think at Children's Services, saying it didn't look like it quite had enough clout to say an EP has been involved, and this is what should happen. I think they looked at the picture and made some kind of comment so that might be something to just bear in mind; if somebody thinks it hasn't got as much weight because it doesn't look like you would expect it to look as a recommendation.

Earlier, we discussed how structuralist education is traditional and adult-driven. Yet there has been a significant shift in education from the draconian picture painted by Dickens, towards a liberal, knowledge-construction approach proposed by Freire. As Katie's head teacher reflects, cultural change is far harder to effect – it takes time and multiple small changes. Therefore, it is important to persevere in the face of challenge, and to work across services in order to promote a deeper understanding of the purpose and practices of person-centred working. While changes to laws and SEND guidance champion such approaches in England and Wales, practices vary widely, as do understandings of what person-centred working means and ultimately looks like. As we found, this can present a significant barrier to implementing changes of this kind at a systemic level:

> **CT:** Going back to [Head]'s point about Children's Services, it is possible that the whole system needs ... if they are not informed, they need to know.

> **Head:** They need to know it is a legitimate format.

CT: They do, and that could be relatively simple to rectify by a communication from [the facilitator]. Do you see what I mean? If it is going to be used by wider agencies, then they need to understand what the paperwork looks like, and what they are looking at and dealing with.

Many of the professionals we spoke to who had attended training in, or observed, a PCR felt that the process and the subsequent paperwork was a sensible way of working and was complementary to the meeting:

SLST: ... it was excellent, really; it just seemed very efficient and that. I do like the way there isn't lots of report writing either. So those pieces of paper, and then with the way they are photographed, and it feels like a very efficient piece of paperwork that comes out that is going to be workable and used, hopefully.

In the spirit of co-construction, the photographs enhance the authenticity of the attendees' voices to be shared, rather than the facilitator paraphrasing what was said. This, we argue, is a key strength of the PCR process, and we should try to retain it when writing the report. Parents also found paperwork very helpful in portraying an accurate representation of views from those involved, as Katie's mother explains:

Parent: ... it's all been kind of verbally, spoken, and you forget by the time you get home; things get forgotten and you don't know what was said and you can't remember. But with this, it was all put on paper and it was there, you know, evidence, if you like, you can see whenever you wanted to. So, if Katie comes up with a question, I can go back to that, and it is there and she can see it.

Katie's mother raised another important issue: the intention that the report be shared with the child. Unlike traditional reports, which may be excessively wordy or complicated, the mixture of visuals and child-friendly language is intended to be meaningful to the child, and not solely to an adult audience. John's mother reflects on how the process of sharing allowed her to help contain John's anxieties beyond the meeting and reassure him about the progress that had been made with the action plan:

Parent: ... we go back to that – something at school comes up that he has mentioned on that report, we get it out and have a look, and we go through what is going to happen and all of these things are happening. So, he understands that it is going to happen and he didn't have anything there [before], he didn't know and would panic more. He would worry more about it, if you like. It's just like getting something off our minds now and we say, OK, we will get this out and check that it is on there, and he knows that something is going to be done as it is in black and white, if you like; it's in front of him, he can see it.

Ownership, and actioning the plan

SLST: ... being told what to do, it was very much through the process of sharing understanding of what was working well and what wasn't working well, and what might help through that shared understanding, and then there were shared outcomes, which hopefully would be engaged with after the PCR.

The action plan will be co-owned by the focus person and the attendees through the process of co-construction. The process of drawing up an action plan within a PCR is a public endeavour. Studies have shown that when a person makes a social commitment to completing an agreed intention or action, completion is more likely and outcomes are optimized. This is probably due to greater accountability to the audience (Gollwitzer *et al.*, 2009; DeBar *et al.*, 2011):

SLST: I think it did really feel like there was going to be ownership in the outcomes, and when that's the case they are much more likely to be followed through. [There was] shared ownership; they weren't our concept, they weren't being imposed, they were genuinely being, I don't know, it felt like the ownership by the people who were going to be delivering those outcomes ...

SENDCo: ... having an EP guide that, and make people say in front of everybody else what they are going to do [is useful]. To give you an example of another PCR ... I had been asking for an FSP to be started by the PSA and I have been emailing, I have been phoning, I have been chasing for over a year, so [it is] really important that we get this in place. She was saying, I'm too busy, I'm too busy, or else just not answering my emails. [Then,] in a PCR, she had to say that in front of everyone that she was too busy to do it, and she couldn't do that because you couldn't possibly be too busy to prioritize this FSP. It was incredibly unprofessional to not prioritize this FSP. So, in front of everyone she had to, in front of everyone, appear unprofessional to them as she had to me in private and she said it would be a really good idea if we had an FSP – job done. So, you know, it shows the power of being transparent.

As the SENDCo observes above, a previous attempt to secure completion in private conversations ended with the professional involved resisting committing to an action she considered important for this family. However, in the public space of a PCR, supported by the facilitator and the information that is derived from the process, she did commit to undertaking the original task and she followed through. Clearly, the sense of accountability and transparency in the PCR requires careful management and support, not least because attendees may feel uncomfortable about the challenges it has raised. PCRs are not designed, and should not be used, to push people into committing to actions they do not agree with. Rather, a PCR should be a supportive process that allows the requests, and the challenges for implementing those requests, to be readily discussed. PCRs should remain collaborative, and not be forceful. The facilitator must balance offering containment with appropriate challenge. Where the situation feels stuck, the facilitator must provide gentle guidance on the process, especially where it relates to his or her own expertise, in order to reach a desirable outcome. This approach is particularly important where there is a history of action plans failing to be followed. This is another argument for the facilitator ideally to be from outside the setting and distanced from the case.

There are cases where the facilitator thinks that a particular action would be the best option, based on their own training, experience, expertise or known evidence base. The authors have been involved in cases where behaviour management has been punitive – such as taking a token away from the child every time they display undesirable behaviour. If the child lost a certain number of tokens, they would not receive the end-of-term treat, regardless of when the behaviour occurred or whether behaviour had improved since. But we know that positive behaviour management approaches, and giving rewards close to the incidence of good behaviour, are far more effective. The facilitator will need to guide the group to think critically about the practice in place, and recognize that they need to move beyond it, without being directive. Nudge theory can be helpful here:

A nudge ... is any aspect of the choice architecture that alters people's behaviour in a predictable way without forbidding any options or significantly changing their economic incentives. To count as a mere nudge, the intervention must be easy and cheap to avoid. Nudges are not mandates. Putting fruit at eye level counts as a nudge. Banning junk food does not. (Thaler and Sustein, 2008: 6)

The action plan must remain co-owned by all those involved, and attendees should not feel pushed into signing up for a particular action, not least because this is unlikely to produce desirable outcomes. One way of doing this is by providing a transparent evidence base for the two or more possible choices and likely outcomes. There are, as we saw, exceptions to this rule, and the facilitator must move between doing with and for the group (Sanderson and Lewis, 2012; White, 2005). Nevertheless, the action plan is the pinnacle of the PCR meeting, and it is this that the attendee usually finds most reassuring. The EP at Katie's PCR comments:

> **EP:** I think because there is a nice clear action plan, and I think that is what people want. They all want to discuss what the concerns are, but what they want to know is, how can they make change and how they can take that situation forward and hopefully make some difference. I think the whole idea of putting together an action plan with time frames around it, who's doing what, and the fact that it is only fed into by what is being discussed in that meeting, I think, for me that gave the meeting a purpose, it gave the meeting quite a clear direction, and it all seemed to feed quite nicely into that action plan. I think that is what service users want, they want to know there is a way forward and there is something they can do to try and elicit some change in a situation they are finding quite difficult to manage.

PCRs depend on the child being at the centre, and understanding and agreeing to the actions that have been set. Studies show that the participation of children in their education increases their happiness, self-esteem and confidence (Davies *et al.*, 2006). Providing collaborative and child-friendly feedback that determines clear goals for the group and what will be done to achieve them enhances the child's sense of ownership, motivation and commitment to be part of that action plan (see Hattie and Timperley, 2007; Hattie, 2008). Individuals are more likely to be committed to actions when they feel they are an influential part of the group (Evans, 2007). When children are given meaningful opportunities to be part of a process, and offered appropriate adult support, they feel connected and more likely to feel ownership, thus optimizing outcomes (Evans, 2007). The PCR process offers this kind of support and, akin to solution-focused brief therapy approaches (for example, De Shazer, 1985), situates the client as having expertise in their own life and what will help them most, and thus gives them a greater sense of empowerment and ownership (see, for example, Henfrey, 2007; Washington, 2016). Katie's mother sums this up:

> Parent: ...Katie is starting to understand now, you know, her own problems, if you like; you know, she knows that she can do something, and I will see her stop and think about what she wrote on the board ...

As Bruner (1996) suggests, teaching the child the tools of meaning-making, and empowering them to take ownership, through understanding their own needs is an important tool in optimizing positive educational and social outcomes. Katie's mother notes how her daughter became a more autonomous agent in her own life because she was given a structure of meaning-making and understanding to scaffold her plan.

Affective experience of a PCR

This was the first PCR meeting for the vast majority of those taking part in our study, so we were interested in capturing what the PCR experience felt like for them and how better to optimize the process. Parents had felt some uncertainty and anxiety around the PCR process at first, their sceptism often fed by past experiences of SEND support processes that had been negative. PCRs are designed to be interactive and to empower attendees to share their views openly, although, as Katie's mother comments, this could be quite overwhelming, particularly when she felt she was underprepared:

> Parent: I then felt uncomfortable because I didn't know what to write and ... I just kept looking at [the pieces of paper] and thinking; I don't know whether it was because I was uncomfortable, I couldn't think straight, or if it was just that I didn't have a clue what to write – it made me feel worse. I did find the questions hard, I did find them hard to answer, as I say; as a parent, you are there because you don't know what to do and you feel you are sort of at the end of your tether with [the school], and for them to say answer questions on what do you think you need, what does this need and what does that need, to then answer them questions, well, if I knew that, then I wouldn't be here. I did feel that a little bit.

Preparation was a major feature of the initial implementation of the PCR process. The questions in the PCR aim to help determine what support those attending think the child needs. Katie's mother felt a sense of disempowerment at the start because she did not have the answers. This was not unusual – it is a sentiment shared by other parents who participate in the PCRs. Therefore, it is important that the parent, and other participants, are offered appropriate support through the process and are well prepared.

People have some solutions to their difficulties; what is needed is a skilled facilitator who will support the group to collectively deconstruct and reconstruct knowledge of the situation, so that ways forward can be agreed. Adequate preparation can help to reduce anxiety by providing thinking time around the questions. However, Katie's mother is a parent who has been disempowered by the education system and who, until the PCR, had felt deskilled and devalued during her quest for getting support for her child. Consequently, her dependency was in danger of increasing, as she began to position herself within a questioning model of assessment (Smale *et al.*, 2000), looking to the professionals for the answers. Parents can be surprised by the sense of increased confidence that a PCR can bring when their child has an action plan to which they have both contributed significantly and agreed. Although some parents said the process felt quite overwhelming at first, it also felt safe and contained. As Katie's mother remarks, it allowed a cathartic release of built-up tension:

> **Parent:** Yes, it was overwhelming, but it was a good overwhelming, you know? What I mean is, it was a kind of release of all my worries and fears, if you like, so it was never worrying in that way.

The release of strong or repressed emotions is cathartic (Veer *et al.*, 2016). We found that such release was of benefit to the parents going through the PCR process. Catharsis is identified by Aristotle in his *Poetics*, where he meant it as a term to describe a cleansing of emotions, and recently cathartic experience has interested psychologists and sociologists (Costa *et al.*, 2014). Working through strong emotions in a safe and contained space with a skilled facilitator can be hugely beneficial.

But as we become more aware of how adults feel going into a PCR, we should not lose our focus on how the child feels. The mother of a child in the early years, Ameera, comments:

> **Parent:** ... from a child's perspective, I think it could probably be a bit daunting. Ameera found it daunting, with all the people, all the attention on her and asking her lots of questions, but maybe an older child may be able to deal with it. I suppose it depends on the individual as well ...

Very young children are offered a child-friendly environment and are generally given toys to play with, as in Ameera's case. Yet the PCR might still feel overwhelming to them. Consideration must also be given to how much of the PCR it is appropriate for the child to attend; as Ameera's class teacher observes:

> CT: I think it is quite a big thing to walk into a room full of adults, some of whom you know better than others, and it's about being aware, as well, of the child's perception of the complicated relationships. If the child is picking up that there is an issue between teachers and parents ... it is kind of more seeing the potential ... to be able to judge it and actually being able to say, 'you can come in for this bit, now you can go off and do your thing for a bit'. Or having them in for longer, [if] that's appropriate, I like the flexibility of that.

As this teacher observes, becoming overwhelmed does not happen only to very young children. What is crucial is to ensure that even young children's views are captured and disseminated to everyone involved in the plan. The teacher also remarks on the ways in which the child may pick up on sensitivities within the room, particularly around relationships. She hypothesizes that if the child picks up on feelings of unease, it might affect the way that he or she feels. This is true of very young people, through to adults, and means that just because Ameera was very young, this does not stop her from picking up on the emotions of adults. The teacher here fears that this might evoke a stress response from Ameera, and others in similar situations. Human communication systems are complex; Symons *et al.* (2016) note that for interpersonal emotional communication to be effective, the understanding of, and response to, the non-verbal expressions and feelings of others is crucial. It is essential that the facilitator has such understanding, and that it is recognized that communication is made and received both consciously and unconsciously among those in the room, and that this can, in turn, influence the way people behave and respond to questions.

When studying group dynamics and how they can play out, Bion (1961) suggested that emotional responses affect not only one's behaviour but also that of others, even when no words are spoken. Understanding group dynamics and how to interpret and respond to them *in situ* is a key skill of the facilitator. Although we do need to take such considerations into account, many of the children we worked with had positive experiences of their PCRs; much of the anxiety lay with the adults. Katie's SENDCo comments:

> **SENDCo:** I was very mindful about Katie's emotional needs in all that, and actually she really went up to the mark – she actually loved it; I can't believe how well she coped with it.

The facilitator must therefore offer containment to adults and organize appropriate support within the PCR, in the form of a PCR champion, so that their anxieties are managed effectively. Some children, such as William and Katie, were also anxious before their PCR; Katie's EP observes:

> **EP:** She was anxious beforehand and she kept quite close to her teacher, her class teacher, who wrote for her. But she, I thought she was quite involved in the process, she managed to go around, I felt she was quite excited by it, that actually she was involved in it. She was able to discuss her views further through the teacher; you could see she was a bit nervous, as she was talking a bit quietly to her class teacher and they were kind of whispering in front of the bits of paper. But she wrote something on every one and she stayed for the meeting ...

Here the psychologist reflects on how, in a PCR she had observed, the PCR champion – in this case the class teacher – helped Katie navigate the process. Preparation activities for the child have also to be in place.

The PCR process aims to empower and give confidence to both the parents and the child, so they can express their views. But it can feel scary and quite exposing at first, particularly for parents. However, as this SENDCo relates, any initial fear is short-lived and the benefits to the child of undertaking a PCR are considerable:

> **SENDCo:** I do think that sometimes, in every aspect of life, you need to go through that rocky part, and as long as you are well supported and not left in that tunnel, you get to the top where you are feeling empowered. That is great, it is how you get to those two places, and making sure that nobody is left feeling exposed, and frightened and alone and worried, really.

It is clear that feelings after the PCR generally outweigh any anxiety the process has evoked. Afterwards, parents said they felt part of the process and were leaving with a far better understanding of how such a collaborative approach ensures that their child will be supported well throughout the programme, as Katie's mother explains:

> Parent: When I look back on it, when I left, to be honest I was
> sweating, I was clammy, I was like 'ohh, get out of there', and
> thought, 'thank god that's all over'. I really was; I don't deal well
> in things like that and I don't like that sort of thing, a lot of
> people. When I got home and I was starting to think about it,
> about what had gone on and what had been said, and I thought
> to myself, 'that's good, everybody thought the same thing'. So,
> yes, I was definitely pleased I had done it … [if] I had maybe met
> [the facilitator] before, it might have been a little bit different.

Although Katie's mother had been anxious during the PCR, the space to reflect on the experience afterwards helped her to see how beneficial the process had been. She also made a good point – that meeting the facilitator before the PCR is a good idea, if it can be arranged:

The benefits of PCRs can extend beyond the setting and carry into the family. John's mother discusses how she has adapted the process to support him with his social interaction and communication needs at home:

> Parent: … it's helping him understand, so if I say something to
> John, now he has got the system to think about where he wrote
> all these things down. We do that at home as well: when he has
> got some worries, I get him to write them down on a piece of
> paper. Because he is writing it down, and then we read it back to
> him, we can work out what he wants to do. So, with a system in
> place, we have now got something we can do at home as well that
> is helping both of us, so we are both getting a lot out of what we
> are doing from that one session.

Knowing that there was a tool she and her son could use together at home gave this mother confidence to work through any worries that John had. However, as we see in the remarks by school staff, her confidence also appears to have come from the transparency of the process:

> CT: I think it was really good to have the parents there to see
> that so many are working together for their child … [it] is really
> valid to see that actually we are all working and fighting hard for
> this child …

> SENDCo: It acknowledges what you have done for the child,
> because sometimes parents don't necessarily see all that in one
> place, do they?

CT: No, they don't. It's not to show off, I don't mean it like that, but it is that everybody is working together for the same goal and for the best for that child.

While this part of the PCR may enhance parents' confidence, it also appears to allow the staff at the setting to communicate effectively about the support that is already in place for the child. And it might also improve home–setting relationships.

So far, we have discussed the child-centred nature of the PCR process, and shown how this encourages the child and parent to engage fully, enhances their confidence and helps towards equalizing the distribution of power. However, it is not always easy to tread the fine line between being child-centred and becoming child-led.

Olivia is a primary-age child who, as part of her needs, struggles with appropriately managing having control – she often seeks or claims control, and then finds it tricky to manage or to deal with having to make choices. The PCR process allows children to take an appropriate degree of control over matters such as how they wish to communicate their views and, within adult boundaries, how the room is set out, the refreshments provided, who is invited and how much of the meeting they attend. Although all of these aspects of setting up a PCR are important, and although the child's positive involvement should be encouraged, risks can arise when adult boundaries are loose or inconsistent. The demands could become overwhelming for the child so that they become more anxious and do not participate, or they could try to seek and retain control after the meeting. In the case of Olivia and the adults who were supporting her in school, the PCR was in danger of becoming child-led instead of child-centred – which can be highly problematic:

> EP: … if I am honest, I felt that we must be child-focused; I felt, at times, we were in danger of becoming child-led in the wrong sort of way. So, we are not there to indulge the child and we do need to make the child feel welcome, but I felt it, it might have been a bit overwhelming for some children to be lavished with so much adult attention in a short space of time …

When Olivia was prepared for the PCR, she requested that pictures and videos of her work in school were shown, along with photographs from home, with her parent's permission. Olivia also requested copious refreshments and snacks. As this was the first PCR the setting had run, all her requests were met, without consulting the facilitator. There are set questions to ascertain whether children might be allowed to choose the refreshments to be provided and whether pictures or videos are shown – these choices should be framed within adult boundaries from the outset. A simple way of achieving this is to offer a choice of two or three possibilities, according to the child's age. Olivia's PCR ran very well, although it somewhat extended and included a refreshment table more like a birthday party than a meeting.

The real difficulty came after the PCR, when Olivia, who did have a primary emotional need, struggled to relinquish her high level of control. Although the matter was addressed swiftly with the help of the facilitator, who was an educational psychologist, it serves as a caution for other PCRs to take account of the dangers of allowing the child unboundaried control. It is also a warning that the setting should first discuss preparation with their facilitator (which is why this was eventually included in the preparation checklist provided in Chapter 3). Finally, it is important to keep in mind that the aim is always to be child-centred, not child-led. It is the duty of care of the adults to set appropriate boundaries that allow the child freedom to exercise a good measure of autonomy, but that also limit that freedom to ensure that everyone is safe and comfortable. This can easily be managed with well-thought-through preparation and communication, so that the PCR is manageable and productive.

Chapter 5

Summary and conclusions

We're changed by the way we live every day
Just look up and reach to the sky
We all have the courage to fly

Andrew Creighton Dodd, Melissa Peirce and
Adam Watts, 'Happily ever after' (2017)

This book has explored a theoretical, political and historical context of person-centred planning to support children who have SEND and their families. We have provided a step-by-step guide to setting up a PCR, and explored the experiences of the process within an educational context with children and families who have an identified or emerging SEND. This closing chapter brings together our conclusions about our work and considers where PCRs can be helpful for supporting children and families. We revisit key points and briefly discuss alternative PCP processes, such as MAPs and PATH.

Situating the PCR

PCRs can be an immensely powerful approach to meeting the needs of children and families. We have tried to show how a PCR might work with specific children, and where it fits within existing local SEND processes. Although we cannot specify where a PCR is always going to be the best approach, it is appropriate in situations where a child's needs are unclear but do not meet the threshold for formal SEND processes, or where there is suspected need but no assess–plan–do–review process in place, or indeed as part of meeting formal SEND demands. Situating a PCR within existing processes is likely to require localized planning, and any trial would benefit from further investigation into the effectiveness of where this process might sit. During our study, we identified five areas where we believe PCRs might work well:

1. **As part of school development or improvement services.** This could be targeted at settings where inappropriate or poorly evidenced requests for formal SEND processes are routinely made. It could also be offered to settings that have identified SEND as an area for improvement through internal evaluations or external inspections. However, the settings most in need might well be those that are least likely to spend

on interventions of this kind. One innovative way to overcome such issues is by negotiating with the local authority for PCRs to become part of their core offer. This is a package of support offered to children with SEND and their families that is funded directly by the local authority, as opposed to being reliant on commissions from individual settings or groups of settings. For example, educational psychologists are well placed to carry out such work, and it would provide a much needed inclusive and preventative approach to meeting certain children's needs. The more complex issue is that which relates to ownership – a local authority may provide PCRs free at the point of delivery, but if the culture of the setting does not align to a person-centred ethos, the outcomes are likely to be poor.

2. **As part of a targeted drive to improve inclusion for specific groups.** In our study, we found that most of those being referred to formal SEND systems were children in the early years, and those who had behaviour and social interaction and communication difficulties. In many of those cases, a PCR sufficed to identify existing good practice, and helped settings plan the steps to take matters forward. This was coincidental and not something we were specifically looking for, so further research would be required to explore the use of PCRs in this way. Nevertheless, PCRs might be helpful as a form of early intervention in such circumstances, and this warrants further exploration.

3. **At the point of request for formal SEND.** If a setting or a parent has requested an education, health and care (EHC) assessment, the local authority must conduct an assessment of need if they suspect the child has SEND. This can generate a high level of formal assessments being undertaken but a low level of Plans being issued. Although this may appear sensible, in reality it blocks access to specialist support such as psychology services, as these are taken up by statutory assessment. So once a referral for formal SEND processes has been received, a PCR would be a useful way of triaging need. A PCR, along with other evidence submitted as part of the request, offers two options to the local authority: (1) the PCR action plan is sufficient to meet need, and the request for a full EHC assessment is refused; or (2) the PCR action plan looks unlikely to meet need, or the child's need is greater than can be reasonably met within the core or local offer. In the latter case, a full EHC assessment is agreed, and the PCR can be used as either a full or partial assessment of need, depending on the professional judgement of those involved.

4. **As part of the educational psychologist's assessment for an EHCP.** If an EHC assessment is agreed, EPs could use PCRs and other person-

centred approaches, as a way of gathering important information as part of their formal assessment of a child's SEND. PCRs place the child and family at the centre of the assessment process and promote co-production of action plans and co-construction of formulations and hypotheses which go on to meaningfully inform any eventual Plan. Additional assessment may be undertaken and fed into the PCR meeting where necessary. This is an important distinction to make; while it is possible to carry out additional assessment *after* a PCR, educational psychologists will often come to a case with initial hypotheses. We have found it helpful to explore these prior to a PCR so that findings can be shared and formulations shaped as part of a team, which can help to reduce power imbalances.

5. **As part of the planning phase of an EHC assessment.** In this case, we assume a formal SEND assessment has been completed, and that it indicates that the child requires an EHCP, but no PCR has been carried out as part of the assessment process. The local authority must write a Plan in discussion with the child, parents and, where applicable, other invested parties, such as staff at the child's setting and other support professionals. Such a Plan could be brought together through a process such as PCRs, but not necessarily exclusively by these means. There are alternatives, such as MAPs and PATH.

Using a combination of these approaches may also be useful, depending on local demand and need. If used in an international context, other legal or political restrictions may also need to be taken into account. Further research in this area would be useful.

We took some time to discuss these issues with our research partners to explore their views on where PCRs might work well locally. PCRs could legitimately be used to support a child as part of early intervention and as evidence of the graduated response required by the DfE/DoH (2015), even if, later on, a request for a Plan is later found to be necessary:

> SENDCo: I think process-wise ... instead of going through reams of paperwork for an EHCP, it is brilliant. Because it is all about what can we do – what can we do that is important now, what are we missing, what else can we do, rather than sifting through reams of paperwork, applying for something that you are not sure you are going to get anyway – [PCRs are] more needs based.

PCRs offer an efficient way of working that prioritizes the person over bureaucratic processes. For example, PCRs do not require a lot of administration, and instead of what is typically a one-off assessment completed by one person, PCRs focus on building on the strengths available in the team around the child, so that they can move forward:

> Participant: ... it was the first one I have done, so I didn't have any expectations. But I think it is a good process because it is kind of aside from the EHCP isn't it, so I think it feels like it is much quicker. It happens there and then and, say, in, what, two hours, and then it is kind of all set in stone, so I think, yes, it is useful.

Where PCRs are used within formal SEND or other established processes, such as FSPs or personal education plans, they will be bound by statutory implications and formats. Finding a way of effectively using PCRs within system-driven processes can be trial and error, and certainly requires patience and creative thinking. Nevertheless, a PCR can offer enough flexibility to complement these processes with some careful planning and collaborative working. As one SENDCo describes, this approach worked well within our study, particularly when it was facilitated by a psychologist:

> SENDCo: ... I think because you have got an EP involved with it, it has extra weighting anyway, because you have got a professional, so it is all good evidence ... I can see how the FSP is more family-based, or it can be, including home, whereas the PCR is more to do just with the child ... High schools might look at applying for an EHCP for them, and I would hope that the PCR supports that process ...

The SENDCo here also reflects the potential for PCRs to be used as a way of satisfying a robust graduated response (DfE/DoH, 2015). However, being a new concept for the local area, some raised concerns around how wider systems might understand PCRs, and whether PCRs would be recognized as suitable evidence for formal SEND processes, if this was required later on. In fact, the process was very quickly adopted by schools as a way of working, and the local authority recognized the potential of PCRs to support all children who had SEND, at least initially. While individual parents, schools and support services continue to invest in PCRs as a way of working, noting the benefits to children and young people, the pull of system-driven bureaucratic processes that attempt to balance dwindling resources with ever increasing demand can quickly engulf even the most rigorous of evidence bases. Nevertheless, support and training of colleagues should always form part of any implementation plan where PCRs are newly introduced.

We saw in Chapter 2 that formal SEND processes are stretched almost to breaking point in the UK. Local authorities are struggling to keep up with demand, and even where a formal SEND process is followed, it often adds little value. The Code of Practice (DfE/DoH, 2015) states that EHCPs should be reserved for the most complex cases, where a coordinated approach and possible access to specialist resources and settings are required. These processes should not be used as an insurance policy – for example, because a child is transferring from early years to primary school. EHCPs should also not be used to access what is already available to settings and the community, nor should they compensate for poor inclusive practice. The DfE (DfE/DoH, 2015) continues to maintain that less complex cases can be dealt with under the local offer. It is in these circumstances that PCRs can be helpful by providing a personalized plan that parents and professionals have contributed to and can action:

> SLST: … certainly, thinking about EHCP requests, I think the idea
> of putting something like PCRs in place before jumping to making
> a referral for an EHCP … I think there can be misconceptions
> about what having an EHCP would do, that actually an awful lot
> can be done with a PCR in terms of getting things that need to
> be done and put in place, without needing to resort to an EHCP.

Here, the SLST reflects on the confusion around what an EHCP might bring to the child. It often includes providing one-to-one support in class, but there is little evidence that such support is beneficial and it may even be detrimental (for example, Sharples *et al.*, 2015) (see Chapter 2). The PCR might help contain anxieties that lead to requests for formal SEND processes, and at the same time meet need. This is because PCRs provide a safe, collaborative space where thoughts and feelings can be explored and proportionate action decided upon.

Parental anxiety is often a strong precursor for formal SEND requests. As we have discussed, EHCPs were seen as a safety net that gave some comfort to parents who could see that schools could be held accountable for supporting their child. But this could lead to disappointment when a Plan did not fulfil expectations:

> OT: I think PCRs are useful for the kids who aren't likely to
> get an EHCP. I think it is useful for the kids and the families
> to do this process, then they will know what is available for

them and what they should be expected to get from both school and professionals. I think some parents are a bit unsure how or whether their kid's needs will be met if they don't get an EHCP or something like that. So I think that is a useful process, and so to get all the professionals involved all at once is useful and it saves parents and the school communicating to so many professionals, which can be quite tricky, this is all done in one.

The OT here reflects some of the parental anxieties discussed, the benefits of PCRs in coordinating a response to meeting need, and the potential to improve communication between those involved in the child's care and education. PCRs are therefore well positioned to be part of a local offer that can help all concerned to pursue formal SEND processes appropriately:

SENDCo: ... I think you begin to embark on the EHCP, you know, what a journey you have got ahead and actually you have got to be really sure that that is the right thing for the child. So, when a parent comes into the school saying, 'is my child likely to need this?' If you can be proactive and say, 'well let's go down this road first, which actually is a slightly shorter road', I think for me that made me feel, as a professional, like I had listened to the parents. I was able to show them that there might be an alternative route, and as a school, we were doing lots for their child and already lots of people were already involved and that the communication was good. So, for me I felt we were listening to the parents, and that I was being very active in helping them feel more confident about the future for their child.

The SENDCo is reflecting on some of the implications of formal SEND processes, and their belief that they should be undertaken from an informed position and a position that is right for the child. This is good practice and falls comfortably within the Code of Practice (DfE/DoH, 2015) so that schools, parents, the local authority and others can work together to improve outcomes for children who have SEND.

Implementing PCRs as part of system change

Earlier we discussed the philosophical concept of structuralism. It is important to revisit this concept in the context of PCRs and the inherent challenges of system change. There is often a hierarchical preference in the assessment and planning for a child. For example, standardized assessments are often assigned greater value than more child-friendly approaches, such as dynamic or play-based assessments. This cultural value is often embedded in systems, most notably in policies relating to SEND or access criteria for education, social care and health services, but is also implicit through the attitudes and behaviours of others. These views are often positivist in nature, assuming that truth is objectively measurable. The professional is given an expert role and charged with helping others to understand the truth by explaining how the problem is maintained and can be resolved.

Person-centred practice stands in contrast to this position. However, as we have discussed, despite legislative changes, which place an emphasis on co-production with children, young people and families, cultural change is incredibly difficult to affect. A range of factors – such as increases in demand, limited resources, continued austerity measures and other pressures – can leave those charged with system leadership to assign resources to address the immediate issue of process management. It is far easier to achieve this goal when complex issues are well defined and those who are directly affected – including children, young people, families and professionals – fall in line with prescribed policies, criteria and processes. For example, formal SEND processes may be linked to additional funding, such as personal budgets or access to other additional financial resources. Although the national picture is mixed, these processes are a result of attempts to manage finite resources that are driven by adult and systemic agendas. Typically, criteria are then developed and implemented by those charged with managing those processes. This can often lead to reductionist, expert and process-driven ways of working, which are arguably more efficient in delivering services and assigning resources. However, an overuse of formal SEND processes may lead to stricter criteria being applied to resource access and incidentally reduce the value of a Plan altogether. This could quite plausibly make such processes meaningless in the long term. Moreover, if unchallenged, these social norms can also become accepted over time and lead to what one might consider as being non-inclusive, expert or process-driven cultures.

Earlier we discussed how the concept of education has positive social norm values ascribed to it, but that it may also be considered a form of social control. In fact, some social norms are constructed in a way that deliberately create social control. Thus, it is important to consider how social norms might be created and maintained when attempting to affect any system change. Knowledge is created through the interactions with others (Burr, 2015). Dominant discourse is often that which is created by those who have the status and resources to exert power (Foucault, 1970), as well as being influenced by cultural values and social history. It is this discourse that provides a basis for policy creation. Policy usually intends to generate particular action – firstly by those who will implement the policy, and secondly by those to whom the policy is put in place to control or order. The extent to which social control is achieved is based on the position of the person or group in relation to the original discourse and associated ideals and action. In our earlier example, we showed how some consider educational policies relating to teaching and measuring of accepted social norms and that this in turn maintains hierarchical subject values, serves ruling classes and gives rise to disempowering SEND rhetoric (i.e. Robinson, 2006; Boronski and Hassan, 2015; Allen, 2017). We have also outlined how process-driven, formal SEND systems can be more easily managed when complex conditions are reduced, usually with some awkwardness, through consistent and ordered ways of identifying, recording and resolving presenting problems. This is at odds with most person-centred approaches and feeds an expert model of practice. Moreover, it supports our argument that new law or policy cannot, in itself, repeal entrenched culture and practices – for example, localized policies and practices may not necessarily align neatly to expectations set in law (e.g. Children and Families Act 2014, Equality Act 2010) or guidance documents (e.g. SEND Code of Practice 2015). This sentiment has been captured in many comments shared throughout this book.

Taking an expert position can therefore lead to a power imbalance between the professional or system and the service user. PCRs intend to redress this, and so it is not difficult to see why some within the system would reject this way of working. For example, as psychologists we have been challenged over how one might formulate a professional view about what is happening in a given situation and how we might go on to report this position following the use of a PCR. In a traditional expert model, one might undertake a range of assessments and consult with a range of stakeholders about a given problem. This serves as a way of collecting information that can later be drawn upon by the professional when writing a report about that situation. Formulation of the problem and how it can be resolved is undertaken, predominantly, away from key stakeholders where psychology is applied *to* the presenting circumstances and a report written to the specification of the system. PCRs focus on shared expertise and co-formulation, where psychology is applied in situ and *with* key stakeholders. For example, a psychologist *may* undertake additional assessment – such as observation, dynamic or standardized testing – before or after a PCR meeting. However, this is not considered privileged knowledge. Rather, it is shared within a PCR meeting *with* key stakeholders where joint formulations and hypotheses are constructed. The psychologist's role is to apply psychology in situ and *with* people to help form and shape ideas about what might be happening and how, ultimately, problems can be resolved as part of a team. This is reported through a child-friendly, co-constructed document (see Chapter 4). As we have shown, co-formulation and subsequent co-production of action plans are profoundly empowering and often welcomed by service users. This is achieved through adapting a de-centred/influential position in our work, and recognizing the need to move between this and other positions as necessary to the wellbeing of the service user (White, 2005).

However, this raises a number of critical questions, such as who is the client and who is the commissioner? What is the relationship between the client and the commissioner? And when can a professional share their expertise and when is it necessary to be in an expert role? With some exceptions, such as safeguarding, there are no easy answers, as context, culture, values and beliefs will vary between settings and practitioners. Moreover, wide contradictions exist, within and between applicable local, national and international law and policy guidance. We believe, in our context, that the primary client is almost always the child, young person or family, as it is for them that we ultimately undertake our work. In the public sector of the UK it is also true that, in the main, taxpayers' money secures those services – whether this is funnelled through local authorities, schools or other publicly funded organizations. The commissioners are those who ask us to complete the piece of work – this is usually publicly funded organizations or, in some cases, privately funded organizations with a social purpose, such as voluntary services. Nevertheless, we anticipate that such services are commissioned on behalf and for the benefit of our primary client(s) and, in the main, are utilizing public or private funds that are designated to be used in the best interests of the person or group the commissioner proposes to serve. We work with these commissioners to negotiate ways in which we can help to move the situation forward, in the benefit of the client and making the most effective use of limited resources and with full regard to our own legal and ethical context of practice. We have also shared throughout this book an evidence base, which we use to guide us when moving into and between expert and non-expert roles, although we also accept that different practitioners will have different views – and our cycle of social norms, values and beliefs begins again. Nevertheless, it is important to remain critically reflective at this level of scrutiny in order to arrive at a decision that feels right for you *and* the client(s).

As we have shown, the issues here are complex and interactive. Indeed, person-centred practice is a term upon which there is little agreement – SoS is considered person-centred by many, but as we have discussed, is quite different from PCRs. Thus, person-centred practice is best considered a continuum, varying depending on different agendas, needs, training and experiences. Moreover, PCRs might not always be appropriate in themselves, and it is sometimes important to use other forms of consultation, assessment or intervention either with or without a PCR.

The PCR as a collaboration

The experiences of PCRs, such as those discussed in this book, have led to an increased sense of partnership and collaboration between settings, parents and other players. In England and Wales, this is a core focus of the Children and Families Act 2014 and associated guidance (that is, DfE/DoH, 2015), and it can be found in political agendas and guidance throughout the world. Many parents with whom we worked commented on how positive the PCR experience was, and how it led to increased confidence for all when facilitated well:

> **Parent:** … before, the teachers weren't making the work easier for her like it needed to be, and although [name of SENDCo] kept telling them, they weren't really listening, and now [name of facilitator] has been in, they are listening. So now that the work is getting easier for her, she is happier, her behaviour is better and that makes me happier, which makes my house a happier place to live in. So, you know, everything, every tiny little thing just makes one massive difference. So I don't feel miserable like I was, because when your child is miserable it makes you miserable … it has obviously made a huge difference.

The PCR process is useful in building such relationships. Our research showed that it enabled the parent's voice to be heard. As this parent says, the potential of a well-facilitated PCR can have a wide-reaching positive impact. Moreover, the voice of the child is centred in the process. We have shown that the flexibility of the process allows the child's views to be gathered and shared through means of communication that are suitable for them, such as drawing, writing, talking, photographs and videos.

PCRs in post-16 education and training

The extension of formal SEND processes means that many local authorities in England and Wales are seeing a significant increase in work with young people who are in post-16 education and training. These young people should still receive access to the local offer, and settings should still endeavour to use this as part of a graduated response to meeting need, ensuring that they collaborate with the young person in making plans. PCRs have been used heavily in the literature to support people moving from children's to adults' services, particularly in social and health care contexts (Sanderson and Lewis, 2012). As this parent told us, careful planning at this stage can help move matters forward constructively:

> Parent: ... we want him to be independent and happy, and leading a life he is happy with, and, you know, as fulfilled as it can be. At the moment William is a long, long way from being able to go anywhere independently or doing anything independent, and at the moment we don't have any links or networks. So, whilst [name of facilitator] was very good at being able to see that and summarizing it for everybody ... [we] are trying to work out what out of the local offer, what can we actually take forward and what support is out there, and that will be going forward in our action [plan] side of things.

This mother makes the point that the PCR can help to identify a starting point for further exploration of the local offer in a collaborative way. However, she raises a particular challenge in post-16 cases, particularly where professionals from health and social care have little or no involvement with the young person, as was the case here. Lack of professional involvement, or cases where professionals are unable or unwilling to engage in the PCR process, can reduce the effects of positive outcomes. Collaboration and engagement in the broadest sense are therefore vital to this way of working.

Alternatives to PCRs: MAPs and PATH

This book has presented empirical evidence of the experience and process of PCRs. There are a number of other PCP approaches that share similar theoretical foundations. We briefly summarize the two that are most often used alongside, or instead of, PCRs: Making Action Plans (MAPs) and Planning Alternative Tomorrows with Hope (PATH).

MAPs (Falvey *et al.*, 2000), designed for future planning, has frequently been used with young people moving into adulthood. A key feature of this approach is that the focus person is solely responsible for inviting people to attend the meeting – as advocated by pioneers of the method. The meeting itself focuses on the future plans, aspirations and goals of the young person, and how these might be achieved, rather than on reviewing current support or making short-term action plans, such as with a PCR. Similarly to PCRs, however, MAPs centres on several key questions posed to the attendees. The meeting centres on the focus person's experiences to date and, while it emphasizes *positives*, *strengths* and *gifts*, it also considers *nightmares* – the situations the attendees and the focus person most wish to avoid. MAPs involves two facilitators, one to facilitate the meeting and the other to draw images to represent the discussion. The second facilitator requires a little artistic skill, as this can make the process more accessible for the child or young person. This is notably different to the PCR, in that the facilitators of the meeting do the scribing, which places them in a more interpretative role. As with a PCR, an action plan is produced by the end of the meeting. It identifies who will action what and when. In the MAPs approach, the action plan is made to achieve the focus person's stated *dream* objective and avoid their *nightmare* scenarios. In this way, MAPs makes objectives much clearer from the outset than a PCR does, and strives to develop objectives through discussion at the action plan stage of the process.

MAPs, like PCRs (especially in the context of our research), considers the facilitator role to be vital. The facilitator should ideally be informed about, but wholly outside of, the context and should not be known to anyone at the meeting. A facilitator should have a solution-oriented, inclusive, positive outlook, and should take account of the expertise that each person brings to the meeting. The ground rules are similar to those outlined in the PCR processes. The atmosphere of the meeting needs to remain relaxed, personal, comfortable and informal.

Planning Alternative Tomorrows with Hope (PATH) has evolved from the MAPs process (Pearpoint *et al.*, 1991). It extends the goals set by MAPs, and aims to determine more detailed actions for both long- and short-term planning. PATH is an eight-step process, which is graphically represented and managed by two facilitators. PATH is more future-focused than MAPs, placing greater emphasis on goals, and the plans that can be put in place to build on the positive and potential support that is already available to the attendees so as to reach those goals. The facilitators work to enrol others in the process, and support everyone to work as a team through confirming constructive relationships and identifying necessary resources along with all those attending. However, PATH works backwards – in the opposite direction to MAPs and PCRs – by defining hopes and dreams for the preferred future, and then identifying the first few steps to achieving those goals. These first steps are an important part of the process as they help to identify the ways in which barriers will be overcome in the immediate future, so the group can effectively move towards the preferred future of the young person.

Our study set out to show how a PCR can be helpful, but we acknowledge that another style of PCP might be more appropriate for certain presenting circumstances. MAPs and PATH, although both tend to use more visuals than a PCR to record the information, still require some degree of engagement by the child. This book has described how the PCR offers an empowering and engaging experience for those involved. The decision about which PCP tool should be used to meet the need of the person who is being worked with should be based on the purpose and need in the presenting situation.

In conclusion

This book has shown that the PCR process, when delivered with care and attention to detail, is an empowering and collaborative experience for everyone involved. Its value lies in providing a space within which school children, particularly those who have existing or emerging SEND, can have personalized action plans developed that lead towards inclusion and optimized outcomes. How a PCR is used will be determined by local need and demand. Grounded as the PCR process is in person-centred theory and ethos, it sits well within the legal frameworks of England and Wales, but can also be suitable in comparable and developing countries throughout the world.

With a focus on greater multi-agency working, service alignment and co-production between agencies, local authorities and parents (DfE/DoH, 2015), the emphasis on co-constructing solution-oriented action plans points to the PCR as a powerful tool available to professionals from a range of disciplines. PCRs have been shown to equalize power distribution among the parties concerned, and consequently to foster a strong sense of understanding, ownership and collaboration among them. Action plans are produced with speed, and are finely tuned to the needs of the presenting people and circumstances.

However, PCRs are not a quick fix, nor are they suitable for all cases. PCRs can be a good starting point in most cases and, for the reasons discussed in the book, can help to repair the possibly fractured relationships between a child's educational setting and his or her parents or carers.

We have found the most successful PCRs to be those that have a family-centred ethos and a child-centred – but not a child-led – focus. As we have shown, this approach tends to promote ownership, and to recognize the power distribution outside the PCR, and the nuanced issues of emotional needs, contextual challenges, and what it means to have vulnerabilities. And it shows that in a well-prepared and well-run PCR, the focus person can still be autonomous and empowered to act as their own agent of change.

How PCRs are used in your locality will depend on many of the issues discussed in this book. It is important to recognize that the research on which this book is based has its limitations, and that transferability of the findings will need to be discussed at a local level. It would also be helpful for further research to be undertaken to explore areas not covered by this study, or to expand upon our initial hypotheses about where PCRs could be effectively utilized.

Despite their limitations, PCRs have a crucial role to play in personalizing education and futures for children who have SEND, and ensuring their long-term inclusion in society. PCRs can be used to teach children about meaning-making, and about how to be autonomous agents who engage in designing their own future and who are active participants in their communities. Whatever their need, these children have the potential to enhance their lives and the world. As the adults supporting them, we are obliged to provide them with the tools that will make this possible.

References

Allen, A. (2017) 'Psychology and education: Unquestionable goods'. In Williams, A., Billington, T., Goodley, D. and Corcoran, T. (eds) *Critical Educational Psychology*. London: BPS Wiley/Blackwell, 15–25.

Allen, G. (2011) *Early Intervention: The next steps. An independent report to Her Majesty's government*. Online. www.gov.uk/government/uploads/system/uploads/attachment_data/file/284086/early-intervention-next-steps2.pdf (accessed 23 November 2017).

ATL (Association of Teachers and Lecturers) (2016) *Are SEND Students Being Let Down? ATL Conference 2016 Resolution 43 report*. Online. www.atl.org.uk/sites/www.atl.org.uk/files/SEND-resolution-43-report.pdf (accessed 14 June 2018).

Augoustinos, M., Walker, I. and Donaghue, N. (2014) *Social Cognition: An integrated introduction*. London: Sage.

Barnes, C. (1990) *The Cabbage Syndrome: The social construction of dependence*. London: Falmer.

Beaver, R. (2011) *Educational Psychology Casework: A practice guide*. London: Jessica Kingsley.

Bellamy, G.T, Horner, R. and Inman, D. (1979) *Vocational Habilitation of Severely Retarded Adults: A direct service technology*. Baltimore, MD: University Park Press.

Billington, T. (2006) *Working with Children*. London: Sage.

Bion, W.R. (1961) *Experiences in Groups and Other Papers*. London: Tavistock.

Bomber, L. (2007) *Inside I'm Hurting: Practical strategies for supporting children with attachment difficulties in schools*. London: Worth Publishing.

Boronski, T. and Hassan, N. (2015) *Sociology of Education*. London: Sage.

Bowlby, J. (2005) *The Making and Breaking of Affectional Bonds*. London: Routledge.

Braun, V. and Clarke, V. (2006) 'Using thematic analysis in psychology'. *Qualitative Research in Psychology*, 3 (2), 77–101.

Bronfenbrenner, U. (1979) *The Ecology of Human Development: Experiments by nature and design*. Cambridge: Harvard University Press.

Broomhead, K. (2013) 'Blame, guilt and the need for "labels": Insights from parents of children with special educational needs and educational practitioners'. *British Journal of Special Education*, 40 (1), 14–21.

Brown, L., Nietupsky, K. and Hamre-Nietupski, S. (1976) 'The criterion of ultimate functioning'. In Thomas, M. (ed.) *Hey, Don't Forget About Me! Education's investment in the severely, profoundly, and multiply handicapped*. Reston, VA: Council for Exceptional Children, 2–15.

Bruner, J.S. (1996) *The Culture of Education*. Cambridge, MA: Harvard University Press.

Burr, V. (2015) *Social Constructionism*. London: Routledge.

Cahn, E.S. (2004) *No More Throw-Away People: The co-production imperative*. Washington, DC: Essential Books.

Carpenter, B. (2007) 'The impetus for family-centred early childhood intervention'. *Child: Care, Health and Development*, 33 (6), 664–9.

Carpenter, B. and Egerton, J. (2005) *Early Childhood Intervention: International perspectives, national initiatives and regional practice*. Coventry: West Midlands SEN Regional Partnership.

Clark, A. (1997) *Being There: Putting brain, body, and world together again*. Cambridge, MA: MIT Press.

Clark, A. and Moss, P. (2011) *Listening to Young Children: The mosaic approach*. London: National Children's Bureau.

Connolly, M. and Gersch, I. (2016) 'Experiences of parents whose children with autism spectrum disorder (ASD) are starting primary school'. *Educational Psychology in Practice*, 32 (3), 245–61.

Corlett, A. and Clarke, S. (2017) *Living Standards 2017: The past, present and possible future of UK incomes*. London: Resolution Foundation.

Costa, N., Faccio, E., Belloni, E. and Iudici, A. (2014) 'Drama experience in educational interventions'. *Procedia – Social and Behavioral Sciences*, 116, 4977–82.

Davies, L., Williams, C., Yamashita, H. and Ko Man-Hing, A. (2006) *Inspiring Schools: Impact and outcomes. Taking up the challenge of pupil participation*. London: CarnegieUK Trust/Esmée Fairbairn Foundation.

DeBar, L.L., Schneider, M., Drews, K.L., Ford, E.G., Stadler, D.D., Moe, E.L., White, M., Hernandez, A.E., Solomon, S., Jessup, A. and Venditti, E.M. (2011) 'Student public commitment in a school-based diabetes prevention project: Impact on physical health and health behavior'. *BMC Public Health*, 11, 1–11. Online. https://bmcpublichealth.biomedcentral.com/track/pdf/10.1186/1471-2458-11-711 (accessed 12 June 2018).

De Bono, E. (1986) *Six Thinking Hats*. London: Viking.

De Shazer, S. (1985) *Keys to Solution in Brief Therapy*. London: Norton.

De Shazer, S. and Dolan, Y. (2012). *More Than Miracles: The state of the art of solution-focused brief therapy*. Abingdon: Routledge.

Deuchar, R. (2009) 'Seen and heard, and then not heard: Scottish pupils' experience of democratic educational practice during the transition from primary to secondary school'. *Oxford Review of Education*, 35 (1), 23–40.

Devecchi, C., Rose, R. and Shevlin, M. (2015) 'Education and the capabilities of children with special needs'. In Sarojini Hart, C., Biggeri, M. and Babic, B. (eds) *Agency and Participation in Childhood and Youth: International applications of the capability approach in schools and beyond*. New York: Bloomsbury Academic, 145–62.

DfE (Department for Education) (2011) *Teachers' Standards: Guidance for school leaders, school staff and governing bodies*. Online. www.gov.uk/government/uploads/system/uploads/attachment_data/file/301107/Teachers__Standards.pdf (accessed 24 November 2017).

DfE (Department for Education) (2015a) *Carter Review of Initial Teacher Training (ITT)*. Online. www.gov.uk/government/uploads/system/uploads/attachment_data/file/399957/Carter_Review.pdf (accessed 8 December 2017).

DfE (Department for Education) (2015b) *The Special Educational Needs and Disability Pathfinder Programme Evaluation: Final impact research report*. Online. www.gov.uk/government/uploads/system/uploads/attachment_data/file/448156/RR471_SEND_pathfinder_programme_final_report.pdf (accessed 8 December 2017).

DfE/DoH (Department for Education and Department of Health) (2015) *Special Educational Needs and Disability Code of Practice: 0 to 25 years*. Online. www.gov.uk/government/uploads/system/uploads/attachment_data/file/398815/SEND_Code_of_Practice_January_2015.pdf (accessed 24 November 2017).

DfES (Department for Education and Skills) (2001) Special Educational Needs Code of Practice. Online. https://assets.publishing.service.gov.uk/government/uploads/system/uploads/attachment_data/file/273877/special_educational_needs_code_of_practice.pdf (accessed 11 June 2018).

Di Leo, J.H. (2013) *Interpreting Children's Drawings*. New York: Routledge.

Dockett, S. and Perry, B. (2007) *Transitions to School: Perceptions, expectations and experiences*. Sydney: University of New South Wales Press.

DoH (Department of Health) (2001) *Valuing People: A new strategy for learning disability for the 21st century*. Online. www.gov.uk/government/uploads/system/uploads/attachment_data/file/250877/5086.pdf (accessed 8 December 2017).

DoH (Department of Health) (2014) *The Adult Social Care Outcomes Framework 2015/16*. Online. https://communitysouthwark.org/sites/default/files/images/ASCOF_15-16.pdf (accessed 5 December 2017).

Douglas, H. (2007) *Containment and Reciprocity: Integrating psychoanalytical theory and child development research for work with children*. New York: Routledge.

Dowling, S., Manthorpe, J. and Cowley, S. (2006) *Person-Centred Planning in Social Care: A scoping review*. York: Joseph Rowntree Foundation. Online. www.jrf.org.uk/sites/default/files/jrf/migrated/files/9781859354803.pdf (accessed 24 October 2016).

DWP/DoH (Department for Work and Pensions and Department of Health) (2016) *Improving Lives: The work, health and disability Green Paper*. Online. www.gov.uk/government/uploads/system/uploads/attachment_data/file/564038/work-and-health-green-paper-improving-lives.pdf (accessed 8 December 2017).

Elfer, P., Goldschmied, E. and Selleck, D.Y. (2012) *Key Persons in the Early Years: Building relationships for quality provision in early years settings and primary schools*. 2nd ed. London: Routledge.

Evangelou, M., Taggart, B., Sylva, K., Melhuish, E., Sammons, P. and Siraj-Blatchford, I. (2008) *Effective Pre-school, Primary and Secondary Education 3–14 Project (EPPSE 3–14): What makes a successful transition from primary to secondary school?* London: Institute of Education/Department for Children, Schools and Families.

Evans, S.D. (2007) 'Youth sense of community: Voice and power in community contexts'. *Journal of Community Psychology*, 35 (6), 693–709.

Falvey, M.A., Forest, M., Pearpoint, J. and Rosenberg, R.L. (2000) *All My Life's a Circle: Using the tools: Circles, MAPS & PATHS*. Toronto: Inclusion Press.

Farokhi, M. and Hashemi, M. (2011) 'The analysis of children's drawings: Social, emotional, physical, and psychological aspects'. *Procedia – Social and Behavioral Sciences*, 30 (2), 2219–24.

Field, F. (2010) *The Foundation Years: Preventing poor children becoming poor adults.* Online. http://webarchive.nationalarchives.gov.uk/20110120090141/ http://povertyreview.independent.gov.uk/media/20254/poverty-report.pdf (accessed 18 December 2017).

Fiske, S.T. and Taylor, S.E. (1991) *Social Cognition.* 2nd ed. New York: McGraw-Hill.

Foucault, M. (1970) *The Order of Things: An archaeology of the human sciences.* London: Routledge.

Fox, D., Prilleltensky, I. and Austin, S. (2009) *Critical Psychology: An introduction.* London: Sage.

Francescato, D. and Zani, B. (2010) 'Community psychology in Europe: More needed, less wanted? *Journal of Community & Applied Social Psychology,* 20 (6), 445–54.

Freire, P. (1996) *Pedagogy of the Oppressed.* Trans. Ramos, M.B. London: Penguin.

Galloway, C. (1978) 'Conversion to a policy of community presence and participation'. Paper presented to the 1978 Regional Institutes in Law and Mental Health, USC Schools of Medicine and Public Administration, Los Angeles.

Geddes, H. (2005) *Attachment in the Classroom: The links between children's early experience, emotional well-being and performance in school.* London: Worth Publishing.

Gold, M.W. (1972) 'Stimulus factors in skill training of retarded adolescents on a complex assembly task: Acquisition, transfer, and retention'. *American Journal of Mental Deficiency,* 76 (5), 517–26.

Gollwitzer, P.M., Sheeran, P., Michalski, V. and Seifert, A.E. (2009) 'When intentions go public: Does social reality widen the intention–behavior gap?' *Psychological Science,* 20 (5), 612–18.

Goodley, D. (1997) 'Locating self-advocacy in models of disability: Understanding disability in the support of self-advocates with learning difficulties'. *Disability & Society,* 12 (3), 367–79.

Goodley, D. (1998) 'Supporting people with learning difficulties in self-advocacy groups and models of disability'. *Health & Social Care in the Community,* 6 (6), 438–46.

Hammond, N. (2013) 'Introducing forum theatre to elicit and advocate children's views'. *Educational Psychology in Practice,* 29 (1), 1–18.

Hammond, N. (2015a) *Forum Theatre for Children: Enhancing social, emotional and creative development.* London: IOE Press/Trentham Books.

Hammond, N. (2015b) 'Making a drama out of transition: Challenges and opportunities at times of change'. *Research Papers in Education,* 31 (3), 299–315.

Hammond, N. (2016) 'Social theatre for social change: The relevance of performance art in educational psychology'. In Williams, A., Billington, T., Goodley, D. and Corcoran, T. (eds), *Critical Educational Psychology.* London: BPS Textbooks/Wiley-Blackwell, 209–17.

Hargreaves, D. (2006) *A New Shape for Schooling?* London: Specialist Schools and Academies Trust.

Hart, R.A. (1992) *Children's Participation: From tokenism to citizenship.* Florence: UNICEF, International Child Development Centre.

Hattie, J. (2008) *Visible Learning: A synthesis of over 800 meta-analyses relating to achievement.* London: Routledge.

Hattie, J. and Timperley, H. (2007) 'The power of feedback'. *Review of Educational Research*, 77 (1), 81–112.

Heider, F. (1958) *The Psychology of Interpersonal Relations.* New York: Wiley.

Henfrey, S. (2007) 'A client-centred evaluation of what people find effective about solution-focused brief therapy'. Unpublished MA diss., University of Birmingham.

Hodgetts, S. and Park, E. (2017) 'Preparing for the future: A review of tools and strategies to support autonomous goal setting for children and youth with autism spectrum disorders'. *Disability and Rehabilitation*, 39 (6), 535–43.

Hogg, M.A. and Vaughan, G.M. (2013) *Social Psychology.* 7th ed. London: Pearson Education.

Jindal-Snape, D. and Foggie, J. (2008) 'A holistic approach to primary–secondary transitions'. *Improving Schools*, 11 (1), 5–18.

Jindal-Snape, D., Vettraino, E., Lowson, A. and McDuff, W. (2011) 'Using creative drama to facilitate primary–secondary transition'. *Education 3–13*, 39 (4), 383–94.

Keenan, M., Dillenburger, K., Doherty, A., Byrne, T. and Gallagher, S. (2010) 'Experiences of parents during diagnosis and forward planning for children with Autism Spectrum Disorder'. *Journal of Applied Research in Intellectual Disabilities*, 23 (4), 390–7.

Kelley, H.H. (1973) 'The processes of causal attribution'. *American Psychologist*, 28 (2), 107–28.

Kelly, B., Woolfson, L. and Boyle, J. (eds) (2008) *Frameworks for Practice in Educational Psychology: A textbook for trainees and practitioners.* London: Jessica Kingsley.

Kelly, G. (1963). *A Theory of Personality: The psychology of personal constructs.* Oxford: W.W. Norton.

Kenny, O. (2016) 'How do young people with ADHD perceive their condition: An interpretative phenomenological analysis'. Unpublished PhD thesis, University of East London.

Kindred, M., Cohen, J., Penrod, D. and Shafer, T. (1976) *The Mentally Retarded Citizen and the Law.* New York: The Free Press.

Kirkman, M. (2010) *Literature Review: Person-centred approaches to disability service provision.* Melbourne: Melbourne City Mission.

Lamb, B. (2009) *Lamb Inquiry: Special educational needs and parental confidence.* Online. http://dera.ioe.ac.uk/9042/1/Lamb%20Inquiry%20Review%20of%20 SEN%20and%20Disability%20Information.pdf (accessed 8 December 2017).

Lewin, K. (1936) *Principles of Topological Psychology.* Trans. Heider, F. and Heider, G.M. New York: McGraw-Hill.

Lightfoot, L. and Bond, C. (2013) 'An exploration of primary to secondary school transition planning for children with Down's syndrome'. *Educational Psychology in Practice*, 29 (2), 163–79.

Lunt, J. and Hinz, A. (2011) *Training and Practice in Person Centred Planning – A European Perspective: Experiences from the* New Paths to Inclusion *project*. European Union: Lifelong Learning Programme. Online. https://www.kvalitavpraxi.cz/res/archive/033/004209.pdf?seek=1527590334 (accessed 13 December 2017).

Mann, G., Moni, K. and Cuskelly, M. (2016) 'Parents' views of an optimal school life: Using Social Role Valorization to explore differences in parental perspectives when children have intellectual disability'. *International Journal of Qualitative Studies in Education*, 29 (7), 964–79.

Mayordomo, R.M. and Onrubia, J. (2015) 'Work coordination and collaborative knowledge construction in a small group collaborative virtual task'. *The Internet and Higher Education*, 25, 96–104.

Measelle, J.R., Ablow, J.C., Cowan, P.A. and Cowan, C.P. (1998) 'Assessing young children's views of their academic, social, and emotional lives: An evaluation of the self-perception scales of the Berkeley Puppet Interview'. *Child Development*, 69 (6), 1556–76.

Meins, E. (1997) *Security of Attachment and the Social Development of Cognition*. Hove: Psychology Press.

Mella, P. and Colombo, C.M. (2012) 'The wheels of change in organizations'. *International Journal of Knowledge, Culture and Change Management*, 11 (6), 247–65.

Morris, J. (1991) *Pride Against Prejudice: Transforming attitudes to disability*. London: The Women's Press.

Mount, B. (1992) *Person-Centered Planning: A sourcebook of values, ideas, and methods to encourage person-centered development*. New York: Graphic Futures.

Murray, P. and Sanderson, H. (2007) *Developing Person Centred Approaches in Schools*. Stockport: Helen Sanderson Associates. Online. www.hsapress.co.uk/PCASchools/pdf/1273319685.pdf (accessed 14 June 2018).

Neal, S. and Frederickson, N. (2016) 'ASD transition to mainstream secondary: A positive experience?' *Educational Psychology in Practice*, 32 (4), 355–73.

Nirje, B. (1969) 'The normalization principle and its human management implications'. In Kugel, R. and Wolfensberger, W. (eds) *Changing Patterns in Residential Services for the Mentally Retarded*. Washington, DC: President's Committee on Mental Retardation, 179–95.

Noelle-Neumann, E. (1974) 'The spiral of silence theory of public opinion'. *Journal of Communication*, 24 (2), 43–51.

O'Brien, C.L. and O'Brien, J. (2002) 'The origins of person-centered planning: A community of practice perspective'. In Holburn, S. and Vietze, P. (eds) *Person-Centered Planning: Research, practice, and future directions*. Baltimore: Brookes Publishing, 3–27.

O'Brien, J. and O'Brien, C.L. (eds) (2000) *A Little Book About Person Centered Planning*. 2nd ed. Toronto: Inclusion Press.

O'Brien, J. and Mount, B. (2005) *Make a Difference: A guidebook for person-centered direct support*. Toronto: Inclusion Press.

O'Brien, J., Poole, C. and Galloway, C. (1981) *Accomplishments in Residential Services: Improving the effectiveness of residential service workers in Washington's Developmental Services System*. Lithonia, GA: Responsive Systems Associates.

Oliver, M. (1990) *The Politics of Disablement*. Basingstoke: Macmillan.

Oliver, M. (1996) *Understanding Disability: From theory to practice*. Basingstoke: Macmillan.

Oliver, M., Sapey, B. and Thomas, P. (2012) *Social Work with Disabled People*. Basingstoke: Palgrave Macmillan.

Osburn, J. (1998) 'An overview of Social Role Valorization Theory'. *The International Social Role Valorization Journal/La revue internationale de la Valorisation des roles sociaux*, 3 (1), 7–12.

Osburn, J. (2006) 'An overview of Social Role Valorization theory'. *The SRV Journal*, 1 (1), 4–13.

Ostrom, E. (1972) 'Metropolitan Reform: Propositions derived from two traditions'. *Social Science Quarterly*, 53 (3), 474–93.

Parks, R.B., Baker, P.C., Kiser, L., Oakerson, R., Ostrom, E., Ostrom, V., Percy, S.L., Vandivort, M.B., Whitaker, G.P. and Wilson, R. (1981) 'Consumers as coproducers of public services: Some economic and institutional considerations'. *Policy Studies Journal*, 9 (7), 1001–11.

Pearpoint, J., O'Brien, J. and Forest, M. (1991) *Planning positive possible futures, planning alternative tomorrows with hope (PATH)*. Toronto: Inclusion Press.

Race, D., Boxall, K. and Carson, I. (2005) 'Towards a dialogue for practice: Reconciling Social Role Valorization and the Social Model of Disability'. *Disability & Society*, 20 (5), 507–21.

Ravenette, T. (1999) *Personal Construct Theory in Educational Psychology: A practitioner's view*. London: Whurr.

Realpe, A. and Wallace, L.M. (2010) *What is Co-production?* London: The Health Foundation.

Reason, M. (2010) *The Young Audience: Exploring and enhancing children's experiences of theatre*. Stoke-on-Trent: Trentham Books.

Robinson, K. (2006) *Do Schools Kill Creativity?* Online. www.ted.com/talks/ken_robinson_says_schools_kill_creativity.html (accessed 7 January 2017).

Rogers, C.R. (2003). *Client-Centred Therapy: Its current practice, implications and therapy*. London: Constable and Robinson.

Roth, J.H., Dadds, M.R. and McAloon, J. (2004) 'Evaluation of a puppet interview to measure young children's self-reports of temperament'. *Behaviour Change*, 21 (1), 37–56.

Sanderson, H. and Lewis, J. (2012) *A Practical Guide to Delivering Personalisation: Person-centred practice in health and social care*. London: Jessica Kingsley.

Scheufele, D.A. (2008) 'Spiral of Silence Theory'. In Donsbach, W. and Traugott, M.W. (eds) *The SAGE Handbook of Public Opinion Research*. Thousand Oaks, CA: Sage, 175–83.

Schofield, G. and Beek, M. (2006) *Attachment Handbook for Foster Care and Adoption*. London: British Association for Adoption and Fostering.

Schwarz, R. (2005) 'The skilled facilitator approach'. In Schwarz, R. (ed.) *The Skilled Facilitator Fieldbook: Tips, tools, and tested methods for consultants, facilitators, managers, trainers, and coaches*. San Francisco: Jossey-Bass, 3–13.

Shapiro, L. (2011) *Embodied Cognition*. London: Routledge.

Sharples, J., Webster, R. and Blatchford, P. (2015) *Making Best Use of Teaching Assistants: Guidance report*. London: The Education Endowment Foundation.

Shoemaker, P.J., Breen, M. and Stamper, M. (2000) 'Fear of social isolation: Testing an assumption from the spiral of silence'. *Irish Communication Review*, 8 (1), 65–78.

Sirsch, U. (2003) 'The impending transition from primary to secondary school: Challenge or threat?' *International Journal of Behavioral Development*, 27 (5), 385–95.

Smale, G.G., Tuson, G., Biehal, N. and Marsh P. (1993) *Empowerment, Assessment, Care Management and the Skilled Worker*. London: HMSO.

Smale, G.G., Tuson, G. and Statham, D. (2000) *Social Work and Social Problems: Working towards social inclusion and social change*. Basingstoke: Palgrave.

Spivack, R., Craston, M., Thom, G. and Carr, C. (2014) *Special Educational Needs and Disability Pathfinder Programme Evaluation: Thematic report: The Education, Health and Care (EHC) Planning Pathway for families that are new to the SEN system*. London: Department for Education. Online. www.gov.uk/government/uploads/system/uploads/attachment_data/file/275104/RR326B_EHC_planning_pathway_-_FINAL.pdf (accessed 8 December 2017).

Spratt, E.G., Saylor, C.F. and Macias, M.M. (2007) 'Assessing parenting stress in multiple samples of children with special needs (CSN)'. *Families, Systems, & Health*, 25 (4), 435–49.

Stephens, L., Ryan-Collins, J. and Boyle, D. (2008) *Co-production: A manifesto for growing the core economy*. London: New Economics Foundation.

Stephens, P., Egil Tønnessen, F. and Kyriacou, C. (2004) 'Teacher *training* and teacher *education* in England and Norway: A comparative study of policy goals'. *Comparative Education*, 40 (1), 109–30.

Stoner, J.B., Angell, M.E., House, J.J. and Bock, S.J. (2007) 'Transitions: Perspectives from parents of young children with autism spectrum disorder (ASD)'. *Journal of Developmental and Physical Disabilities*, 19 (1), 23–39.

Swain, J., Finkelstein, V., French, S. and Oliver, M. (1993) *Disabling Barriers – Enabling Environments*. London: Sage.

Symons, A.E., El-Deredy, W., Schwartze, M. and Kotz, S.A. (2016) 'The functional role of neural oscillations in non-verbal emotional communication'. *Frontiers in Human Neuroscience*, 10, 1–14.

Thaler, R.H. and Sunstein, C.R. (2008) *Nudge: Improving decisions about health, wealth, and happiness*. New Haven, CT: Yale University Press.

Thatcher, M. (1987) *Interview for* Woman's Own *('no such thing as society')*. Online. www.margaretthatcher.org/document/106689 (accessed 20 May 2017).

Thomas, G. (2008) 'Facilitate first thyself: The person-centered dimension of facilitator education'. *Journal of Experiential Education*, 31 (2), 168–88.

Thomas, G. (2010) 'Facilitator, teacher, or leader? Managing conflicting roles in outdoor education'. *Journal of Experiential Education*, 32 (3), 239–54.

Tickell, C. (2011) *The Early Years Foundation Stage (EYFS) Review: Report on the evidence*. Online. www.gov.uk/government/uploads/system/uploads/attachment_data/file/516537/The_early_years_foundation_stage_review_report_on_the_evidence.pdf (accessed 8 December 2017).

Turnell, A. and Edwards, S. (1999) *Signs of Safety: A solution and safety oriented approach to child protection casework*. New York: W.W. Norton.

United Nations (1924) *Geneva Declaration of the Rights of the Child*. Online. www.un-documents.net/gdrc1924.htm (accessed 10 November 2017).

United Nations (1948) *Universal Declaration of Human Rights (217 [III] A)*. Online. www.un.org/en/universal-declaration-human-rights/ (accessed 10 November 2017).

United Nations (1989) *Convention on the Rights of the Child*. Online. https://www.ohchr.org/EN/ProfessionalInterest/Pages/CRC.aspx (accessed 29 August 2018).

Unsworth, K.L. and Clegg, C.W. (2010) 'Why do employees undertake creative action?' *Journal of Occupational and Organizational Psychology*, 83 (1), 77–99.

Veer, E., Ozanne, L.K. and Hall, C.M. (2016) 'Sharing cathartic stories online: The internet as a means of expression following a crisis event'. *Journal of Consumer Behaviour*, 15 (4), 314–24.

Washington, C. (2016) 'Exploring the use of strategies to support Solution Focused Brief Therapy (SFBT) to enhance engagement with adolescent males: One counsellor's experience'. Unpublished MA diss., University of Canterbury.

Weiner, B. (1979) 'A theory of motivation for some classroom experience'. *Journal of Educational Psychology*, 71 (1), 3–25.

Weiner, B. (1985) 'An attributional theory of achievement motivation and emotion'. *Psychological Review*, 92 (4), 548–73.

Weiner, B. (1986) 'An attributional theory of achievement motivation and emotion'. In Weiner, B. (ed.), *An Attributional Theory of Motivation and Emotion*. New York: Springer-Verlag, 159–90.

West, P., Sweeting, H. and Young, R. (2010) 'Transition matters: Pupils' experiences of the primary–secondary school transition in the West of Scotland and consequences for well-being and attainment'. *Research Papers in Education*, 25 (1), 21–50.

Whitaker, S. and Porter, J. (2002) 'Valuing people: A new strategy for learning disability for the 21st century' (letter to the editor). *British Journal of Learning Disabilities*, 30 (3), 133.

White, J. and Rae, T. (2016) 'Person-centred reviews and transition: An exploration of the views of students and their parents/carers'. *Educational Psychology in Practice*, 32 (1), 38–53.

White, M. (2005) *Workshop Notes*. Online. www.dulwichcentre.com.au/michael-white-workshop-notes.pdf (accessed 23 February 2017).

Williams, A., Billington, T., Goodley, D. and Corcoran, T. (eds) (2016) *Critical Educational Psychology*. London: BPS Textbooks/Wiley-Blackwell.

Williams, H.M., Parker, S.K. and Turner, N. (2010) 'Proactively performing teams: The role of work design, transformational leadership, and team composition'. *Journal of Occupational and Organizational Psychology*, 83 (2), 301–24.

Wolfensberger, W. (1969) 'The origin and nature of our institutional models'. In Kugel, R. and Wolfensberger, W. (eds) *Changing Patterns in Residential Services for the Mentally Retarded*. Washington, DC: President's Committee on Mental Retardation, 51–179.

Wolfensberger, W. (1995) 'Social Role Valorization is too conservative. No, it is too radical'. *Disability & Society*, 10 (3), 365–8.

Index